Rev. Francis R. Davis
Our Lady Of Lourdes
120 Fairmont Road
Elmira, N. Y. 14905

THE YES BOOK

An Answer to Life

JOSÉ DE VINCK

THE YES BOOK

AN ANSWER
TO LIFE

FRANCISCAN HERALD PRESS
ALLELUIA PRESS

BY THE SAME AUTHOR :

THE WORKS OF BONAVENTURE SERIES
Five volumes translated from the Latin
Franciscan Herald Press, Chicago Ill. (Distributors)

THE VIRTUE OF SEX
Original hard-cover edition, Hawthorn Books Inc., New York,
1966 and 1967. Exclusive distributor : ALLELUIA PRESS
Spanish paperback, Ediciones Paulinas, Madrid, 1968
Italian paperback, Edizioni Paoline, Rome, 1969
American paperback, Abbey Press, St. Meinrad, Indiana, 1970

THE CHALLENGE OF LOVE (With Reverend John T. Catoir, JCD)
Original hard-cover edition, Hawthorn Books Inc., New York,
1969
American paperback, Abbey Press, St. Meinrad, Indiana, 1971
Spanish paperback, Ediciones Paulinas, Madrid, 1971

BYZANTINE DAILY WORSHIP (With Archbishop Joseph Raya)
Original hard-cover and paperback editions, ALLELUIA
PRESS, 1969

Second printing 1974

Library of Congress Catalogue Card Number : 77-190621

ISBN : Hard cover : 0-911726-12-8
        Paperback : 0-911726-11-X

Published by :
ALLELUIA PRESS - Box 103
    Allendale, N.J. 07401
and : Combermere, Ont. Canada

Printed in Belgium

ACKNOWLEDGMENTS

THE QUOTATIONS in this book that serve as illustrations of the text were collected by the author in the course of many years for his own information and without any publishing intention. Tracing the precise sources of all of them has proved practically impossible. Permission to publish has been requested from the publishers of recent material. If any other texts published here are copyrighted, the author hereby apologizes for their use and requests the kind permission of copyright holders. Any assistance from readers in spotting the exact sources would be appreciated.

Permission has been obtained from the following publishers :

Alfred A. Knopf, Inc., for two quotations from " Markings" by Dag Hammarskjöld, New York, 1964, copyright Alfred A. Knopf, Inc., and Faber & Faber, Ltd.

The Center Magazine, Box 4068, Santa Barbara, California, 93103, for excerpts from article by Dr. John R. Silber.

All quotations from the French are in the author's own translation.

I was abandoned to a thousand thoughts, and since many days, had attempted mightily to discover myself and what was good for me, and what evil to avoid, when suddenly— was it myself or was it another, I do not know, and that was precisely what I ardently sought to know. Anyway, it was said to me, " If you find what you seek, what will you do with it? Who will you entrust it to before you die? " I answered, " I will keep it in my memory. "—" But can your memory keep everything your mind has perceived? "— " Indeed, it cannot. "—" You must write, then.... Ask for strength, then for help so that you may find what you seek; then write it down, so that this child-bearing of your heart may quicken it and make it strong. Write only the results, and spare the words. Think not of the crowd that may read these pages : a few will understand. "

AUGUSTINE OF HIPPO
Opening lines of " The Soliloquy "

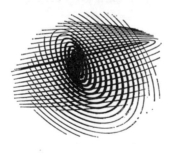

TABLE OF CONTENTS

Behind the demands of youth for relevance and the demands of the elderly for law and order is the human concern for meaning, for a life that makes sense. JOHN R. SILBER

" The day of the Lord " on which the Enthroned One " arises, " and for terror and for rapture reveals his kingdom, which was the hidden meaning of creation from the beginning, is, in the power on the prophetic vision, this very present day. MARTIN BUBER

Our ignorance of ourselves has a specific nature : it results neither from the difficulty of obtaining the necessary information, nor from its inadequacy or rarity. On the contrary, this is due to the very abundance and confusion of the notions humanity has gathered about itself in the course of ages; and also, to the division of ourselves into an almost infinite number of fragments by the sciences that have shared the study of our body and our consciousness. ALEXIS CARREL

That which was the best in the past is not so any more, for it lacks conformity with God's will which is now running through different channels to give birth to the duty of the present instant. And it is this duty, whatever its appearance, which is the most sanctifying for the soul. J. DE CAUSSADE

Every creative philosopher is a hidden theologian. PAUL TILLICH

FOREWORD

PERHAPS WE REACH our ripest old age somewhere about twenty, when the world seems to weigh on our shoulders and we don't quite know what to do about it; when our thoughts awaken to the burden of truth to be known, and our hearts to that of love so little loved. At that age, many of the more thoughtful among us go through a crisis of universal melancholy often expressed by a word so Germanic I don't have the heart to use it here.

At the ripe age of twenty, there is in the depth of eager and pure minds a pressing desire to change everything for the better, to convert all of humanity at a single blow, replacing everything sick and decayed with something new and fresh and lively.

On the one hand, the young are faced with a world sorely in need of their help; on the other, they must admit their own unpreparedness and grope among dozens of revolutionary theories, each one of which claims a better world as its goal. Because of the resulting confusion and conflicting programs, and also because of the manner in which philosophies and theologies are generally presented, students may be tempted to give up the struggle for truth. The young and eager are in constant danger of becoming the old and weary, in both body and spirit. Involved too soon without training or principle in the jungle of real life, they may become cynical, seeing their future as a free-for-all, with no other rule than strong-man-wins and no other goal than immediate material gain.

Can we blame them? Has any clear and practical example of right behavior been given to them, any effective hope for a better way of life, any constructive synthesis of an improved personal and social order, any program of enlightened, positive, generous contribution they themselves can make to happiness and peace in the world?

In most universities, there seems to be no coordinated program that would form the whole man, no attempt at bringing together the many glimmers and glimpses of truth taught in widely separate courses, no balanced system providing realism for the idealist, idealism for the realist, encouragement for the disappointed or sound judgment for the imprudent. Teaching seems to be highly specialized, attempting to inject masses of pre-digested data into brains treated as if they were electronic computers—and not the most refined instruments of life and love which they are.

Too often, students are offered philosophy in the form of impersonal analyzes, and theology, in that of dogmatic and apologetic demonstrations expressed in a language foreign to their minds and hearts. What they need is to be in contact with thinking individuals surprised in the act of thought, and loving individuals surprised in the act of loving God. Wisdom and truth, then, instead of receiving lip service, will be seen as constituting the meat of life.

The foremost task of any institution of learning is not indoctrination, but education. Teaching is not a filling of tanks, but an opening of avenues. It is essentially a matter of human relations, of one man passing on the best of his inner visions to others, so that they in turn can go beyond his dream. Every campus, then, should have men sufficiently detached from themselves and from the ambitions of the world to be totally attached to others and to the needs of the world, men with such a spirit of wholeness and holiness that it becomes contagious.

There is at present a powerful revival of interest in philosophy and theology. Under the influence of pressure from below, universities seem to be developing these subjects at a rate that would have seemed unbelievable a few years ago. Courses in theology for laymen are multiplying. An actual begging for substantial food is being heard and answered on many a campus, and reported in the daily press, echoing one of Salinger's characters who complained that he had been studying philosophy for years, but had never been offered wisdom.

The present book is launched as a modest attempt along this line of thought. Its essential characteristic is a firm belief in the unity of wisdom. Psychology, philosophy and theology should not be treated as subjects so distinct they almost never meet. On the contrary, they are mutually illuminating. This book, then, is an introduction to existential wisdom. It is offered with the hope that it has something valuable to propose to the present peace-loving, truth-loving and love-loving generation.

J. de V.
Easter, 1972

I Don't know who—or what—put the question, I don't know when it was put. I don't even remember answering. But at one moment I did answer to someone or something YES, and from that hour I was certain that existence is meaningful and that, therefore, my life, in self-surrender, had a goal. DAG HAMMARSKJÖLD

Saintliness: a shifting of the emotional center towards loving and harmonious affection, towards " yes, yes, " and away from " no. "

WILLIAM JAMES

" Yes, That, the Real, " this is declared to be the triple name of Brahman.

THE BLESSED LORD'S SONG (Hindu)

....and yes I said yes I will Yes! JAMES JOYCE

YES! A ZEN MASTER

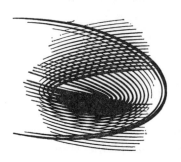

The future of humanity lies in the hands of those who are strong enough to provide coming generations with reasons for loving and hoping.
Our era needs such wisdom more than bygone ages if the discoveries made by man are to be further humanized.

VATICAN II
" The Church in the Modern World "

While there has been much talk about the information explosion, there has been no explosion of wisdom.

PAUL WOODRING

Wisdom is a harmony of knowledge, will and feeling, and by no means necessarily grows with the growth af knowledge.

BERTRAND RUSSELL

What those growing up so desperately need is a human being who will take them from where they are, who will believe in them to such an extent that they also will come to believe.

GABRIEL MORAN

It is important, desperately important, that we accept our youth for their idealism and that they accept us for our experience.

JOHN R. SILBER

They (the students) want not only well-ordered, carefully delimited lectures and texts,... but also a philosophic correlation of the branches of knowledge, a relating of these to viable ideals and commitments.

JOHN JULIAN RYAN

There is between you and me a kind of mutual calling, a double questioning about the sense of life, an expectation of some reciprocal revelation that will be given to us, an awaiting for some miraculous help we will offer each other.

LOUIS LAVELLE

INTRODUCTION

INTELLECTUAL AND SPIRITUAL UNREST are a sign of hunger. Many questions are now being asked by many minds. In the absence of clear answers, the craving for truth is intensified. Where, then, can we find the key to worthwhile belief? How shall we know what to do with our lives? Intelligent men and women are filled with interrogations about themselves and others : whence, and how, and whereto, and always, why, why, why? If such questions could be given proper answers and people were willing to act by them, happiness would reign instead of anguish, freedom instead of oppression and peace instead of war. Such a state of affairs, of course, would be quite utopian, but something at least can be done right here and now for the fostering of happiness, freedom and peace, AND THE ONE TO DO IT IS YOU. But how do you go about it? What is wisdom, and can it ever be attained?

There are no short-cuts, no ready-made answers. Every man and woman must go, slowly and painfully, through the full process of personal civilization, from primitive childishness to responsible, enlightened adulthood, realizing finally that the complete and perfect human being is the one who loves in spirit and in truth and transmutes this love into daily action.

The problems of personal life may be reduced to these three :
— The PSYCHOLOGICAL : Who am I?
— The PHILOSOPHICAL : What is truth?
— The THEOLOGICAL : What is love?

PART I

THE PSYCHOLOGICAL PROBLEM
OF PERSONAL LIFE

Who Am I?

To be born simply initiates a life-long process of coming alive.
WILLIAM TOOHEY

*There can be no communication between people until they
have actually become people; in order to be able to give
himself, a man must have taken possession of himself in
that sorrowful aloneness without which nothing is ours and
we have nothing to give.* LOUIS LAVELLE

*God gave to some animals the speed of flight, to others
claws, or wings : but he has so disposed man that he, God
himself, is his strength.* JOHN CHRYSOSTOM

*Your essential duty and desire is to be united to God. But in
order to be united, you must first of all be.*
PIERRE TEILHARD DE CHARDIN

Every human being is a unique wonder.
FRIEDRICH NIETZSCHE

*What I am myself is based on my original relation to
Transcendence : in defiance and in surrender, in falling
away and in soaring up, in obedience to the law of day
and in the passion of night.* KARL JASPERS

CHAPTER 1

THE PERSON
AS AN INDIVIDUAL

KNOWING YOURSELF IS A PRIVILEGE

WHO AM I? Many *uninitiated* people go all the way through life and reach the gates of death without ever having asked the question. Their consciousness is barely sufficient as a means of survival. It reacts defensively to external provocations in the immediate present. It is entirely used up by the necessities of food, warmth, air and clothing—with a little left over, perhaps, for love. Even this love is often semi-conscious : it may at times rise no higher than instinctive affection for mate and offspring. Those who live on this level are confined to an earthly Hades deprived of vistas and perspectives. The most shattering splendors of heaven and earth leave them untouched, unchanged, unmoved. They may reach high levels of wealth or authority and yet remain completely deaf, blind and insensitive to all that counts. They may be in appearance the most successful millionaires, the most glamorous and envied sex-goddesses, or dictators endowed with the power of life and death—and yet in terms of truly human value, they are not there at all. They stare with unblinking eyes right into the face of the sun, and see nothing. Quite often, they are not unhappy : they just don't know of any other way of life, and they would be brutally cruel to anyone who would try to change their routine. The *initiated* may wonder at their plodding : they gaud them, shake them, try to wake them up, only to produce wonder at first, then whimpering, then an explosion of destructive fury. *

The mere fact, then, of being able to stop and consider, to ask the question, " Who am I? " is the proof of a highly privileged state, a luxury of civilization that is not open to all.

* See excerpt From George Santayana, p. 189.

How can we stop? Nothing is easier. There is no need to take
a month off or retire under some shady bower. All we have to do
is to switch for a few moments from some trivial or perhaps even
damaging occupation that may be consuming our time, and concentrate instead on our true needs. To be alone and thinking about
ourselves is neither egotism nor narcissism : on the contrary, if
moments of solitude are used in the right spirit, we may very soon
come to realize how much we need the help of others, how totally
unable we are to fulfill ourselves without external assistance,
how intolerable life would be without the close, warm and immediate
company of those we love.

There is a deeper problem for those who cannot love, who by
reason of some wound or refusal have lost the means of pleasant
communication, outgoing concern for the welfare of others, the joy
of sharing in the human give-and-take. Some people have been
so badly hurt they are unable even to receive love, let alone give it.
They cannot believe that they themselves are the worthy objects
of true, sincere, generous and pleasurable love. They are so much
on the defensive that they grow claws and horns and armor-plated
hides. They have failed to realize that the only way to sanity is
a defenceless acceptance of life, a dropping of swords, a dismantling
of dungeons.

Perhaps the most amazing feature of man's evolutionary success
is the fact that he has survived unarmed, smooth-skinned, weak,
slow, earth-bound, in a world of beasts that had every physical
advantage over him. In spite of such handicaps, he became their
undisputed king. Why? Because he has the one thing the beast
lacks : intelligent love. But intelligent love must be put to work
lest man fall back to a level lower than the beast.

It is through intelligent love that man has been able to prosper
in the small community of the family, in the tribe, the city, the
nation and the world. It is through isolation, distrust violence
and war that he is courting his own destruction. His only enemy is
himself.

Once again, then, the first result of a return into self is awareness
of the necesity of going out to others in order both to receive
and to give. To receive : we should seek the right counselors, read
the right books, discover through the lives of the truly great what
are the nature and means of true greatness. Human perfection will
then be seen to consist in transparency, luminosity, simplicity,

childlikeness, openness, concern, attention, perseverance, trust, warmth—and unrelenting effort toward the true and the good. This is a far cry from the more obvious characteristics of popular idols : the star, the leader, the millionaire. Yet, there is no contradiction between perfection and success. The star may be truly gifted, talented, generous, doing well what he or she is called upon to do : giving pleasure, uplifting the spirit, making the spectator rejoice and applaud, adding the very much needed spice of fancy to a world threatened with dullness and mediocrity. The star may also have every one of the virtues that constitute human perfection—from transparency to warmth. The same is true of the leader and the millionaire : they too may be saints, although the temptations of wealth and power may make it harder.

MAKING THE MOST OF WHAT WE HAVE RECEIVED

NOW THAT we have had a chance to look into ourselves, to be alone with ourselves and to understand our need of others, let us go back to our origin and consider how we began.

Every new " I, " every man and woman that is born comes into the world—or rather, as we shall see, " out" of the world—as the result of an act of love. The conscious purpose of that act is just that, love, and nothing else—the manifestation of the powerful passion to be joined to a mate in the sexual act. The natural outcome—the producing of offspring—is not considered during the performance of the act itself, nor in most cases is it a determinant of it. People generally make love for the sake of making love, and not for the sake of making a child. The fruit of love is often a surprise—a gratuitous emergence from the intimate union of man and maid. We are then the indirect fruit of love rather than the direct effect of any genital intent. The child is both gratuitous and unique : in it, there is a new combination of life, an untried complex, an entirely novel and unexpected justaposition of genes.

Every child comes into the world with a physical body it has received from its parents. No one has any choice in this matter. No one has anything to say about his or her sex, hormonal balance, blood type, genetic pattern or inborn qualities or defects, any more than about the degree of natural intelligence and sensitivity that depend upon the physical development of the brain and sensory organs. Nor again is anyone responsible for the damage inflicted by diseased or ill-fed parents, or by parents suffering from alcohol or drug addiction. The new-born child is totally unable also to prevent such accidents as oxygen starvation, forceps distortion, or any other trauma at birth. In fact, so numerous are the possible obstacles to the formation of a physically and mentally normal child that every one appears as a kind of natural miracle. On the other hand, there are powerful built-in mechanisms of normalcy and survival. The human body, even that of an infant, is incredibly tough, for it has been trained by millions of years of evolution to survive even in the most difficult circumstances.

Physical obstacles are far from being the only ones that meet a child at birth : it may also be assailed by defective emotional or mental attitudes of parents, tribal groups or local society. A child, it seems, may be affected adversely even before birth by an emotionally upset mother who rejects it in advance, living in a state of defensive indignation against the " intruder. "

The most important period for the development of personality seems to coincide with the first few months after birth. It makes all the difference if the physical world is first revealed as a place of warmth and tenderness, or as one of cold isolation in which the infant is left alone to struggle through the first terrifying experiences of living. Instead of opening out, of flowering in the sunshine of love, the slowly forming mind will then build for itself a well-defended refuge. The pattern of the dull, self-centered, unseeing, autistic man or woman is being set.

The same dangers are present at every age. As the child grows into self-conscious adolescence, there is added the further risk of rational damage : the distortion of judgment and thought. At this point, however, the process may be reversed, for the passive and irrational manifestations of childishness may be overcome through growth of the autonomous will. Traits may have been formed, bad habits developed in the irresponsible age, but they are reversible provided they appear on the surface of the conscious mind, and the proper methods are used to counter them.

All of us are more or less damaged. No one ever develops with total smoothness along the lines of ideal love and perfect truth. All of us, then, must come to know where we stand and what we should do. At this point, when the possibility of self-creation is discovered, it is most important to answer the question, " Who am I?" This is the first step in the awareness that we are not yet what we are supposed to be—and the first incentive toward finding out what it is. This is the gate to possible redemption, to the discovery of what is truly human. If the question is not asked, or asked improperly; if it is not answered, or answered in the wrong way, there is great danger of falling to the level of the living dead who have never risen to the challenge of meeting themselves. In such cases, and in the absence of corrective measures, all the early negative influences will be free to follow their evolutionary course and reach their natural conclusion : the dead-end of the non-participant, deprived of faith, hope and love.

By contrast, if the question is asked and answered properly, there is no cause for despair, even for the most badly hurt. On the contrary, it may be those who have been most severely battered by circumstances beyond their control who will come out on top as soon as control becomes possible.

" Who am I?" Yes, I am this imperfect creature, pushed around by an apparently blind destiny, born to this world without having chosen to be born, brought to life and reared by parents I am forced to accept, endowed with a body over whose physical, sensorial and mental mechanisms I have had so far no power at all. But now is the time when the true " I " appears, now is the time " I " can begin to do something about it.

My parents may have been good, bad or indifferent : I had no choice as to their inner virtues—but I do have a very clear choice as to my relations with them. Whatever their objective worth, I may act positively toward them. Depending upon who they are, this action may be an expression of admiration, love, understanding, ndulgence or compassion : all of these attitudes are constructive and have a positive effect on the development of my inner self. In the case of inadequate parents, instead of revolt and antagonism, I can try cooperation in whatever measure is possible. Instead of saying " NO! " as an automatic measure of self-defense, I can try saying " YES! " and try offering even more than what is asked of me. Instead of hiding in a tower of contempt, I can go out, not half way, but all the way. The results may be astounding.

So many parents are afraid of their children, afraid because unsure. They are afraid of being seen through, because they are only too clearly conscious of their inadequacy. Fearing rejection, they do not dare to communicate. You, then, should go out to them; you know so much more than they do! You should try at least to talk things out with them. Tell them your dreams—in which they will recognize those of their own youth; explain your viewpoint and try to understand theirs, thus reaching a common ground that is always present as long as love survives.

WILL YOUR ANSWER BE YES OR NO?

WE ARE complex beings. The body never acts alone; physical acts go together with emotional involvement, intellectual awareness and moral responsibility except on the very lowest level, that of automatic physiological functions. And even they can have an influence on the spirit which depends entirely upon a healthy body for its proper activity.

The simplest physical act produces sensations, inner feelings of motion. It also becomes the occasion for receiving various reactions from the outside world to which we cannot be insensitive : we must react in some way or other. These messages come to us as pleasant or unpleasant; they make us aware of the many beings that exist beside us; they force us to respond affectively.

This may be in either one of two ways : closing or opening, rejection or acceptance, refusal or offering, YES or NO. As the body is in need of exercise and fresh air under the threat of atrophy and asphyxiation, so is our emotional being in need of positive response : the contact of love. It needs communication in order to become rich and to extend beyond the limits of self-feeling.

But human experience is not limited to the physical and the affective : there is also the rational and its apex, the spiritual. Affective experiences force upon us judgments of value; on the basis of what we love, we must plan the possible roads of action, know the world around us and figure out in our own and personal way what we are going to do. This is the beginning of the tremendous adventure of thought. By the grace of the built-in powers of our body, our sensory perception and our mental capacity, all of the highest forms of life belong to us as our birthright.

Now is the time to pick up the infantile " I " and try to make something of it. The difference between success and failure rests upon the proper use of freedom. Until now, I have been almost entirely dependent upon others. My only form of self-assertion may have been revolt against authority. Since I am now free, the only authority against which to revolt is myself—and the house that contends against itself is bound to fall. Instead of revolting against what I am, why not try to bring into being what I can be? It is my major work. Instead of majoring in English, Chemistry of Computer Analysis, why not try majoring in ME?

At any moment of their lifetime, man and woman are made up of a composite picture of what they have received through heredity and what they have made of it through the use of intelligence and free will. What they have received is unchangeable; what they can make ot it is infinitely variable. And so, there is available to all of us a constant possibility of development in any of an infinite number of ways, a chance of becoming really our own personal selves, overcoming ever-more perfectly any obstacle we may have met at birth or in our later life.

At no time in history has there been a more refined and intelligent humanity; never before was there offered such a chance to try out every avenue of vital endeavor; never has mankind been better equipped for success. Right here and now, you and I living as individuals in this second third of the twentieth century are immensely valuable elements of an adventure in research and progress that was not even dreamed of by earlier men. The question is, then, what are we going to do with ourselves?

The individual cannot become human by himself.

KARL JASPERS

Our destiny never ceases to develop itself through those states ever so minute that fill each day. They may often be so insignificant as not to reach our consciousness, and to make us believe they leave no trace in the world.

LOUIS LAVELLE

Every second is a moment of decision, for the better or for the worse. ERICH FROMM

Now I am not what I was when the word was forming to say what I am. WILLIAM CARLOS WILLIAMS

Man's freedom is not freedom from conditions but rather freedom to take a stand on whatever conditions might confront him. VIKTOR E. FRANKL

Man has survived through tenderness. LOREN EISELEY

Man, when alive, is soft and tender; when dead, he is hard and tough. All living animals and plants are tender and fragile; when dead, they become withered and dry. Therefore it is said, " The hard and the tough are parts of death; the soft and the tender are parts of life. " LAO TSU

All fragments must be gathered; all the complexities of the puzzle of life, which is so perplexing to so many, must be fitted into a pattern of meaningful beauty.

CATHERINE DE VINCK

CHAPTER 2

THE PERSON
IN THE WORLD

THE WORLD OF MULTIPLE CHOICE

WE ARE ENDOWED with physical, emotional and rational powers, but they are of no great use to anyone, and least of all to ourselves, unless they are developed, organized, disciplined and made to flower in acts of true adult creativity. This must be achieved in the midst of the present world : we must take it as it is before trying to improve it.

Except for rare moments of isolation and silence, we are being constantly assaulted from all sides. Every one of our senses is active in some way, consciously or unconsciously. We are living under a shower of data that sparkle and clatter around us, impinging upon our external defenses, entering our field of perception, invading our thoughts. In the modern mechanical space age, impressions are multiplied and accelerated. The rhythm of machines hastens the pace of life, adding immensely to the challenge offered to both the senses and the mind—but also making it ever more difficult to survive as personal beings.

It is in the midst of this apparent chaos that we are to remain free and to become wise. A free man is a man able to choose. A wise man is a free man able to make the right choice. A saint—and I don't mean a plaster saint of holy superstition, but a fully developed human being—is a wise man who has made the right choice. But where and when can we choose? Where and when do we have a chance to assert our freedom, accept or refuse, do something positive that will affect the course of our life?

There are some major instances of choice that are clear to all : the selection of a field of studies, a career, a husband or wife. These are so important that their effect on our future does not need to be stressed. But there are many other instances of choice that may not seem important, and yet leave their mark : the choice of a car, of house furnishing and equipment, of clothing, books or works of art, of a place to go on vacation, etc... All this depends upon people's personal taste and contributes to the formation of their style of life. In such matters, there is a clear risk of being over-influenced by advertizing or by the crowd, of following the fashionable trend at the expense of our real good, of locking ourselves in the format of some in-group instead of making up our minds about what is best for us within the objective circumstances of our means and the subjective height of our ideals.

There is also an infinity of smaller acts, almost unconscious and automatic, such as meeting a parent or acquaintance, reading a book, driving a car, eating, drinking, or just being alone for a while and doing nothing in particular. These, too, are occasions of free acts the sum of which influences what we are. Unless there is here some basis of reason, there is in these many actions no possibility of forward motion in any precise and fruitful direction. As someone said, " Going from anywhere to anywhere leads to nowhere in particular." There is, then, a fundamental need of knowing where we are going, and why, and of establishing on these premises a clear pattern of action. Perhaps it cannot be established in full at the very awakening of rational life : yet, it must be thought out consciously as soon as possible, and developed progressively as the years go by.

If there is no program, no preplanning based on a clear scale of values, our actions will not rise above the level of instinct : we will remain the slaves of some irrationally acquired set of habits, responding automatically to the loudest and most immediate claim and pursuing thoughtlessly what seems to be our most immediate good. We will be tossed about at the mercy of impressions that assail us constantly. We will be tumbled and confused and confounded as one more of the anonymous and useless pebbles on a barren beach, tossed to and fro by a tide they cannot understand. There may be movement in some direction, but it will be passive, and the result may be the exact opposite of our true vocation, of what we could have accomplished through conscious effort.

Passivity breeds impersonality and mental death. The damaging process may be invisible, for heedless rushing prevents clear vision and patient thought, the only remedies to self-destruction. Passivity and the pursuit of the wrong kind of goal are often combined, for by passively submitting to the pressures of the moment, a man easily forms the habit of surrender, and surrender is the consequence of defeat.

Every living man or woman is in a state of constant flux, changing from one condition into another. The change may be almost imperceptible while it is going on, unseen to the subject even after a total transformation over the years. And yet, it is visible to others. We all know the feeling of surprise when meeting an acquaintance after a long separation : " My, how changed he is, so bitter and disappointed. " Or, on the contrary, " Hasn't she mellowed wonderfully?" We are moving constantly, either up or down—and generally in one way after the other—as erratically as the stock market. We cannot possibly remain what we are : only the dead are motionless.

Whence such changes? They are the combined effect of countless choices, the residue of major or minor acts that have affected our perfectibility or our liability to decay, for we are able to move to incredible heights and depths. In any field of endeavor, any normal human being, by dint of good planning and persevering effort, can rise to astounding levels of skill. Some such skills are so common as to be hardly noticed, and yet they are near-miraculous. Take for instance the simple fact of typing these notes. If a writer attempts to analyze the total operation involved in the elaboration of an idea, its expression in the words of a given language, its transposition into graphic signs, the instant selection of these signs on a keyboard, and the reception and understanding of them by the reader, he will fall into depths of wonder.

CHOOSING HOW TO SERVE

THE BALANCE of a civilized economic system rests on an exchange of services. When each citizen specializes in a particular aspect of some useful service which he can provide at a lower cost than could his neighbor, this same neighbor will not go to the trouble of doing things his own hard way : he will spend part of his earnings to procure the service of the specialist. In some instances, the neighbor is totally unable to do the thing himself. Exchanges of specialized services occur on every level, from garbage collection to electronic engineering, from baby-sitting to post-graduate teaching.

The important thing for you is to choose your own speciality, to determine what particular mousetrap you will develop so as to have the world beat a path to your door. Some people are naturally limited : they soon reach the ceiling of their possible development and cannot aspire to activities of the higher rank. They are not inferior morally or spiritually : some of the greatest saints were extremely simple souls. What you must do, then, is obtain an objective appraisal of your own level of intelligence. This is best done through tests and counseling. An important indication will be what you like to do. You will always enjoy doing what you do well, and you will be able to discover in this way the direction of your possible development. Once this direction has been determined, there is only one course of action : singleminded, persevering, long-lasting work.

The mind needs to be furnished with the wisdom acquired by other men, to assimilate what has been done before in the field of its choice. However, it should absorb procedures rather than facts, methods rather than results : it should be educated as a producer rather than indoctrinated as a reproducer. A foreman may know every detail of a machine and have experienced every one of its possible uses— but it takes an engineer to design a better machine.

The important thing is for each man and woman to select the right skill, and the reason why it is important is that they have only a limited amount of time and energy, so that every minute wasted on some useless activity is an irrevocable loss of what could have been.

There is no need here for tenseness or anxiety nor for a meticulous accounting of time. We will indeed be held accountable for every one of our words and actions, but we are under no obligation to make the right choice unfailingly and to bring it to perfect fulfillment. All that is expected of us is the right disposition, the development of a set or progressively assimilated tendencies that will lead us almost effortlessly to the correct choice. In older terminology, this is called "virtuous habits", and, as Father Pierre Charles, S.J., said so well, " in the depth of all true virtue there is a magnificent and royal lightheartedness. "

The point to be made here is that these habits—either of order and wisdom or of disorder and folly—are both the cause and the effect of our acts. They are the cause in that whatever we do is influenced by our dispositions of the moment; the effect, in that these dispositions are the result of countless decisions made in the past.

Some people hope to have their falterings excused under the pretext that they could not help doing what they did, that they were impelled irresistibly. But responsibility goes much further than the actual committing of an act : it also covers the formation of habits that made the act possible.

If responsibility were limited to the act, a man could excuse himself from a crime by claiming that he had been compelled beyond the limit of resistance of his will. In fact, he is guilty because he is responsible not only for the act itself but also for the development of the bad habits that made it unavoidable.

That is why it is so important to know what we are doing in the world, even in seemingly unimportant matters. *We need to be conscious of who we are and where we are going, otherwise we have no chance of becoming anything but drifters, followers of the common destiny instead of the makers of our own.* Undirected freedom will produce nothing but a garden of weeds and tangled vines, an ever-darkening confusion that ends in despair.

Contemporary literature and show-business are cluttered with the stories of such wasted lives. Despair, anxiety, *la nausée*, perhaps these are the most widespread diseases of our time. Little seems to be done to overcome them. Millions of dollars are spent to heal physical ills; other millions go to wasteful wars or to providing material necessities, food, clothing and physical health. Men now live longer in our country than they did even twenty years ago. But the extension results often in nothing more than stretching the period of vacuum of the elderly, postponing the solution of death, giving frustration an opportunity to grow into helpless revolt. Few things are more depressing than an old peoples' home, or the false front of a " Golden Years Resort. "

Frustration and despair are not limited to those who have lost the fight and grown too old to do anything about it : disappointment and defeat accompany us at very step. They are with the schoolgirl submitted too soon to the pressure of social competition whose early years, instead of being a peaceful road to the flowering of intelligence and judgment, now change into a rat-race toward some College utopia. The young man in business or industry, the young woman in society—not only Society, the Vanishing Myth, but also the most sub-suburban group of neighbors—are all vying for achievements which, when attained, will still leave them unsatisfied. Presidency of the local Bridge Club or P.T.A., a job promotion, the latest sports car or fashionable outfit are no more soul-satisfying, and no less, than the presidency of the United States or the fortune of Henry Ford : they actually have nothing to do with truly human happiness.

THE CONDITIONS OF SUCCESS

HUMAN happiness, greatness and holiness may be achieved in any state whatsoever, for their substance is quite unrelated to external circumstances. Once a human minimum of security, shelter, food and drink are assured, the conditions of happiness are a matter of the heart and spirit. In fact, they are totally unrelated to the conscious and unconscious goals of nine tenths of the people around us who are seeking mostly things that will do them no good.

Many a "successful" man has managed to make his life so unbearable that there was no other solution than to end it.

Does this mean we should give no attention to the things of the world and concentrate all our energies upon some future life in the hope it will give us everything we missed on earth? Should we go through the present life with a pinched face and eyes tightly closed to beauty, pleasure, glamor, sex? Should we forget about ambition and wealth and power, and retire into some cave, exchanging our Brooks Brothers and Balenciagas for sack cloth? Not in the least! And yet, why not at least indulge in some few periods of true penance, true solitude, true renouncement and simplicity—if for no other reason than to find out who we are and where we are going, and to gain a better appreciation of what we have? Periodic reassessment is a necessity in any long-range planning. The span of our life is such that we cannot keep running on the momentum of our first impulses, of our first ideas of success. We must stop and consider : life is not a dream. It is all too real, but if we never take a long, cool and careful look at what we are doing, it may very well turn into a nightmare.

Only then, only after careful re-evaluation of our past and replanning of our future can we make of the years to come something better than a progressive sinking into despair. The important thing right now is to have asked the question and sought the answer : to have realized that the semi-conscious, subhuman pursuit of just any conventional goal, the adoration of some hastily gilded idol, may not in cold fact coincide with what we are or what we should become. So let us at least try to seek solutions to some of the major problems of life.

Perhaps one of the first questions is this : Do we have a chance? Has anyone ever succeeded in this earthly enterprise of human life? The answer, without any doubt, is YES. Some men and women do enjoy a quality of living that is above anything that may happen to them, and makes them stand out with particular warmth and brilliance. These people are seldom the popular heroes or even the canonized saints : they are much too happy to attract official attention. Many of the modern heroes are the artificial product of the advertizing industry, and are often very far from leading happy personal lives—and a number of canonized saints would not make our preferred list, for the standards by which they were approved were strange and narrow. Let us call these truly successful men and women the "Lovely People" by contrast with the conventional "Beautiful People" of society and show business. These lovely people live among us in a manner that somehow seems superior, more worth-while, more deeply rewarding. They have eyes to see and ears to hear, and a heart to love. They are generous, peaceful, undisturbed even in their misfortunes. They live with an intensity of feeling and understanding that leaves the ordinary man with a sense of longing if he is kind, and of envy if he is not. He wonders how they have become what they are. Was it through a gift, a hereditary quality, a natural power of perfection and enjoyment—or by dint of personal effort?

The same question in reverse may be asked of other people, the failures, the misfits, the vandals, the hawks : were they born that way, or are they slowly working toward their own destruction?

Between these two extremes, there is the mass of the lukewarm, the half-alive, the slobs : those who have more or less given up on faith, hope and love. Were they born within fences out of which it was impossible to escape, or have they entrapped themselves?

The answer to all such questions is of utmost importance, for upon it will depend an attitude either of fatalistic surrender or of active and hopeful self-improvement. This answer, as in the case of all vital matters, is neither simple nor easy to find, and it may be different in each individual instance. Yet, if no attempt toward a solution is ever made in relation to individual destinies, the automatic result will be an increase in the number of the ugly, the bland and the living dead.

At this point, no generalization will do; no sweeping abstract principle will serve as a sufficient guide. The problem is of man, and the solution will have to be by and through him. Even for the Christian, there is no ready-made, God-given solution to the challenges of daily life. Revelation itself, both in the Old Testament and in the New, is a constant reminder that *we* are in charge of the world even if the supreme government is God's. Providence, then, may be seen, not as a *deus ex machina*, some theatrical trick that will undo man's blunders and set things straight, but as a mysterious and almost imperceptible inner power that works as a silent guide to individual consciences, and only for those men and women who are willing to listen. The very first condition of true awareness, then, is to be open, to seek, to develop the realization that we, as individuals living here and now, are responsible for the world as it shall be.

Those who never seek, never listen, and therefore have no inkling of their responsibility, are drop-outs of life. Their number is large, and it includes sub-groups :

— *The mentally underprivileged :* These bear no blame, for they could not have attained the understanding of what is wrong with the world and how they could improve it. Society has a duty to support them, as it supports its infants.

— *The uneducated :* Here again, society is in charge. If the social structure of government, ruling classes and institutions of learning functions in such a way that some elements of the population are neglected and bypassed when they could have been educated, the blame rests, not on the victims, but on those in power; and the sin is no less serious for being one of omission; and the sinner could be you who read this book and I who write it.

— *The improperly educated :* Here we come across mixed responsibility. Many teachers, generally without malice, offer a philosophy of life devoid of faith, hope and love. Many students, instead of pursuing the road of faith, hope and love, branch out into the back-roads and sewers of learning, or end up by devoting their lives to worthless or even damaging jobs, from the tobacco industry to advertizing frauds, all the way to racketeering and crime. Most of these people have the mental equipment and education to know better.

The mentally underpriviliged lack the natural gift of listening to the secrets of wisdom. The uneducated were denied their chance. The improperly educated bypassed or actually refused that chance.

Lovely people, then, are found only among the sufficiently gifted and properly educated. This is not a moral judgement, nor does it exclude the many people who have been denied a formal education, and yet have lifted themselves up by their own means. But only the gifted and properly developed have a chance of gathering an aura of human perfection, for they alone have sought, and listened, and found out what was worth the effort of their living.

But how did they do it? How did they get to be lovely? Even when we do possess a reasonable amount of natural intelligence, it may have been assaulted by adverse circumstances : inadequate parents, ill health, provincialism, bigotry—the list extends to

every human misery. All this may be overcome, for the only important thing is to have kept the spark alive : the living embers of
hope in a better life for oneself and for others. As long as a flicker
of this light remains, there is the possibility of developing it into
a glorious blaze. The horror of slum-living consists precisely in this,
that in spite of the extraordinary resiliency of the human spirit,
the flames of faith, hope and love are knocked out so constantly
and monotonously that nothing is left but despair and revolt.
Violence may be seen sometimes as the final, desperate flaring of
the fire of life.

As long as the flame of hope, faith ond love remains alive, there
is also an urge to listen and to seek : listen to the inner voices of
conscience, and seek the ways and means of perfection; and this
is the Art of Life.

THE UNDERPRIVILEGED AND THE OVERPRIVILEGED

ART is in the order of action. It consists, according to Thomas
Aquinas, in doing well what needs to be done. It requires the
knowledge of what to do, the will to do it, and the perseverance to
continue until results are achieved. Like every other art, the art of
life consists essentially in a series of choices, a succession of acceptance and rejection of possibilities after they have been rationally
weighed; in the fashioning of an object : ourselves, and the world
around us.

We are often dependent upon external circumstances that restrict
our freedom. We are born in a specific milieu, live as part of a given
social group, in which we are reared and educated. Most of the

elements that influence our life, beginning with the first impressions of infancy, tend to fix us in our original environment. Our future may be determined in great part by our parents' wisdom, imagination and spiritual wealth—or by the lack of them. Two factors, however, tend to make us different, to break us out of the mold of conformism : a very unhappy youth spent in revolt against adverse circumstances, and a very happy one that has resulted in unhampered development.

Many homes seem to be made up of people who have surrendered in defeat. They may have started out with high hopes and dreams, but after bashing their heads against social class rules, job classifications or lack of humane working conditions, they have surrendered to the overwhelming demand of providing bed and board for themselves, their mate and their brood—at any cost to their deeper desires. There is nobility even in this, for the goal itself is praiseworthy. Astonishingly beautiful flowers of humanity may often grow in such gardens of mediocrity. Truly loving and intelligent children will be able to save their initial newness and originality. The future lights and leaders of mankind may be found in a row house, or on lower-suburbia's Main Avenue. All they need is a kindling of whatever is left of their fire, enough guidance to allow them to grow above their surroundings, enough faith and love to persuade them that they can make it to the top of human worth and human wisdom. They need to be awakened to the fact that the world is considerably larger than the perspective of some lower social group. They need guidance from teachers and counselors who will save them from mediocrity and prepare them for some truly worth-while task.

The difficulty, however, is that the less privileged areas—those precisely in need of the best teachers—often have inferior schools. Underprivileged children are frequently taught by underprivileged instructors, maintained in their own prejudices, and thus deprived of a chance of ever discovering what life is all about. Where it would take tens of thousands of teachers of great wisdom and holiness to save the children, there are tens of thousands of teachers who, in spite of much effort and good will, lack the qualifications needed for such a tremendous task. There are not enough good teachers to go around, but more of the better ones should devote their talents to improving the schools of the underprivileged. It is one of the major duties of our time.

With the wealthy upper classes, the problem is different. A life made too easy and permissive creates an artificial athmosphere of facility that fails to correspond with the harsh reality of the world of the suffering. To a youngster born in a middle-class residential neighborhood, educated in a " good" school and graduated from an Ivy League University, the fact of human misery may be totally unknown. Not only is he amply provided with the necessities and luxuries of life : he seldom, if ever, comes in contact with anyone who is not. He may have heard about slums without ever having seen one; he may not have the slightest idea of the working conditions of the unskilled; he will go through town from restaurant to bar without ever seeing the inside of a kitchen, without ever dreaming of the existence of a human dishwasher. The world as he knows it exists only on the polished side of the swinging doors.

Such unconsciousness goes a long way toward social irresponsibility. The home athmosphere may be one of refined dilettantism, a truly cultured life—but the complete absence of concern for the welfare of the underprivileged, the systematic rejection even of the thought of a suffering humanity, make such a life worthless and unreal.

There is something revolting in the atrocities of the French revolution of 1789, and of the Bolchevik uprisal of 1917. But both the French *Ci-devant* and the members of the Czar's court—absentee landlords, exploiters of the peasants, decadent and self-centered profiteers—richly deserved to be punished for their social crimes. The flippancy and unawareness of the secure is best exemplified in the well-known anecdote about Queen Marie-Antoinette, the wife of Louis XVI, who was to die later on the scaffold. When she heard the poor were starving from want of bread, she is said to have enquired wonderingly why they didn't eat cake. The same socially explosive situation and the same abuses as those which led to the French and Russian revolutions seem to be developing under our very eyes in some South American countries, not to mention our own.

By contrast, a number of great families here and abroad have placed their power and their wealth at the service of the intellectually and spiritually hungry. Sometimes this represents a belated compensation by the sons for the unscrupulous business methods that brought wealth to their fathers. This, however, is better than the self-centered greed of other rich families that are content with taking all they can without doing anything more for the common welfare than the signing of an occasional deductible check to silence the murmurs of a dying conscience.

This is one point where the younger generation can take over. It has already demonstrated a superb scorn for the trappings of the rich. A real sense of solidarity and mercy seems to be developing among them. May it prosper and spread fast enough and far enough to prevent any future social upheaval.

So much for the idle rich. Now about the wounded, those young people of all classes whose childhood and youth have been damaged by poverty of body, emotions, and spirit. These are the slum children, the minority children, the ghetto children—but also the offspring of the rich, of broken homes and unloving parents, of parents unable to solve their own emotional, intellectual or religious problems who have passed on their frustrations to their children.

The result in the next generation is generally revolt and bitterness, an uprising against authority in any form. Resentment may come to such a boiling point that it is manifested in anti-social attitudes and actions.

Yet, young people in this painful state may be seen as having a better chance than the overfed : they are not numbed, or unconscious, or absent. On the contrary, theirs is a raw and wide-awake presence. They have lived under stress, they have been challenged, their desires and appetites have been whetted—in contrast with the rich who have tried everything and found nothing but disgust. The underprivileged have seen injustice and borne in their hearts a great desire for right. They are vital, tense, hungry, lean, ready for adventure, like the barbarians at the doors of decadent Rome. The important thing is to channel these powerful forces along the ways of good.

Instead of each wounded soul recoiling in its own shell of pain, let suffering men and women come out in the open and begin to do something about injustice, not by destroying the social pattern that is hurting them, but by building up a better one, beginning at the roots through a concerted action upon the people they meet : first upon themselves, then upon friends, then, through progressive, patient and tolerant action, upon those responsible for their pain. This applies as well to Civil Rights workers as to migrant farmers, to the victims of broken homes as to the financially oppressed. Their very state of victimhood gives them a living power, a vital contact with the core of human life that may be used to rebuild first themselves, then society, through the might of their patiently acquired but dynamic experience.

Now, for the happy few born and reared in a loving family, in a spirit of freedom and kindness, of light-handed discipline and deep personal care. The question here is different. There is also need of adaptation to the outside world, for when home life has been harmonious and happy, it is all too easy to imagine that this other world is peopled with intelligent, kindly, creative, lovely men and women, and to treat everyone as if he were gifted with such virtues. The consequent rebuffs and disappointments may come as a severe shock to the innocent. It is then all too easy to pass from a rosy, optimistic and unrealistic outlook to one of scorn, and to snob the world because it is not up to our standards. The result may be confinement within a narrow group of holier-than-thous, the building of protective walls around one's own perfection, and its preservation within an isolated dungeon against the assaults of life. Such an attitude was characteristic of an erroneous view of spiritual life in the middle ages, and is still seen in our days.

In such a reaction, there is little wisdom and no merit whatsoever. For we are in this world, not for the purpose of saving our personal souls through indulging in isolation and contempt, but for the sake of the common ascent of humanity, for the *pleroma*, the glorious fulfillment of the universe as a whole; for the forwarding of the Kingdom, for the growing and maturing of something infinitely greater than ourselves.

If we were brought up in a family where the fires of love were burning brightly, it is our duty to communicate this warmth, and not to preserve it as a privilege or a means of personal comfort. In order to establish a true communication of love, we must see the world, not as the despicable " other " of Jean-Paul Sartre, but as our own neighbor, part of ourselves, of our being and our destiny. " My brother is my life, " wrote a monk of Mount Athos.

Let the happy go out to the needy and share their happiness with them. And the needy are not only the financially underprivileged, but perhaps much more the dumb, the dishonest, the unkind, the unimaginative, the ugly. Perhaps they have a right to a reward greater than ours : did they ever have the chances we received at birth?

STANDARDS, RIGHT AND WRONG

WHAT, now, are the circumstances in which we live? What is our social and economic milieu? It is characterized essentially by the quantity of available money. Our needs, real or induced by publicity, are growing constantly. The artificial provocation to buy, the extreme facility of credit, tend to disrupt completely the distribution of personal income into channels of relative importance. The distortion is more apparent, perhaps, among the less educated classes where the symbols of wealth assume a much greater importance than actual well-being. A shiny Cadillac may often be seen next to a shack that is lacking in elementary comforts, or a large color TV set in a two-room home. But the trend of illogical buying is not limited to the lower classes : many a home in suburbia is a beautiful shell, completely lacking in furnishings and actual necessities.

A society based on money suffers directly because of the exaggerated importance attributed to it. When all energies are devoted to getting more of it, with very little thought being given to its proper use, money-making becomes the major pursuit, the absolute that may be seen to justify the means. The consequence is the so frequent exploitation of the weak. Excepting the case of the few honestly rich by their own merit or talent, most rich people in our society have become so through blood-money : through the slave-driving of industrial giants, the fruit of the work of countless drones accumulated into the pockets of a few very rich. On the next level, the not-so-rich offer their lives and their substance to the tribal custom of keeping up with the Jones. The poor, lacking any chance of living a truly human life, pay for their mere survival.

On none of the three levels—the rich, devoured by the drive to preserve and increase their wealth, the not-so-rich consumed with one-upmanship, and the poor compelled to do or die—does there seem to be any margin of energy left over for the real business of living. Who has the time for play, relaxation, meditation? Even play is expensive, over-organized and frantic. Who can still afford to live at a pace sufficiently slow, sufficiently adapted to the refinements of perception and thought, to be fully and humanly satisfying?

The temptation, then, is great to give it all up : to retire from the immediate, pressing struggle of our imperfect world and seek refuge in solitude. Some solitaries retire because of pride and disgust : their aloofness is a form of self-exaltation, an expression of scorn for the hoi-polloi, a search for egotistic salvation, sometimes even a misplaced search for God. Such men and women exist both in the religious life and out of it—and all they deserve is our pity.

But there are also true contemplatives : men and women who retire from the external pressures and pleasures of the world in order to do something positive, loving, active, for the benefit of others who continue to carry the burden of the day. They are not shirkers : in fact, they may be carrying much more than the average load. They are not self-seekers : their sacrifice is not intended for their own glory, but for the labor of love, the continuous, purposeful effort of the assistant to suffering mankind.

To conclude : We are born as we are in the world as it is. This world was made by those who came before us. We are, then, faced with the choice of going along with all its imperfections, or doing something more than giving a damn; giving ourselves to the permanent task of building a better world for ourselves and our children.

Man must achieve wisdom before he can use his knowledge.
                                                    LEWIS MUMFORD

*In many souls a hunger and thirst exist which can be satis-
fied only by the printed word. Between the eager reader
and the writer, who should also be eager, a current of
sublime charity may flow, since there is giving and receiving
on both sides.*   ERNEST HELLO

*For our perfection we need to be vitally savage and mentally
civilized; we must have the gift of being natural with
nature and human in the society of men.*
                                            RABINDRANATH TAGORE

*Today, in the age of an affluent society, most people suffer
too few demands rather than too many.* VIKTOR E. FRANKL

CHAPTER 3

THE PERSON
IN THE STATE OF GROWTH

EDUCATION VERSUS INDOCTRINATION

ALL LIVING BEINGS are constantly changing from within. Biochemical processes follow their course from birth to death; sensorial perception waxes and wanes; the intelligence moves from primordial ignorance into relative states of understanding. The latter is generally the result of education.

The first question in matters of education is to make a distinction between what needs to be done and much that is actually wrong in current procedures. The contrast will appear in a comparison between true education and indoctrination.

— Education consists in drawing out the potentialities of an untrained mind; indoctrination, in stuffing it with ready-made recordings.

— Education is fundamentally the teaching of principles; indoctrination, the forced memorization of facts.

— Education is a dynamic process influencing and developing the whole being; indoctrination, a static cramming of the memory.

— Education is a liberation of the individual's latent powers; indoctrination, the enslavement to pre-existing prejudices.

— Education lifts up by helping an individual reach above himself; indoctrination debases by limiting a man to the following of another's will.

— Education leads the spirit freely to truth; indoctrination confuses it, vainly attempting to formulate what is beyond words.

— Education is a joyful discovery of the inexhaustibility of life; indoctrination is the drudgery of collecting fossils.

— Education stems from the desire to share happiness with others; indoctrination, from the vanity of man's false wisdom.

— The teachings of education are gathered from life-experience; those of indoctrination are found in any encyclopedia.

The problems of education are a concern of the parents and educators rather than of the young, for how can untrained minds know how best to train themselves? Only on the university level does the conscious mind of the student develop to a sufficient degree of self-determination to choose in a rational way the direction of its evolution.

People should be expected to have reached the age of reason at least by the time they must choose their way of life. It is one of the most important decisions a man or woman will be called upon to make. Seldom does it depend upon a single act of the will; it consists most often in a chain of decisions the ultimate consequence of which will be to place a man where he is. In many cases, these many influential decisions are not made with the required awareness and intent : people often drift into one occupation rather than another by the simplistic process of following the easiest road each time they come to a dividing of the way. From minute step to minute step, they walk in a certain direction, suddenly to realize they are stuck in a place where they did not want to go.

As indicated above, the future of many is determined in large part by the ways and habits of their tribe. Furthermore, by the time career-determining decisions must be made, few people dispose of the mental equipment for rational choice. It is quite impossible to establish universal rules, since all such matters are highly individual, but a few suggestions may be useful.

As soon as you are able to determine the field of your own personal ability, investigate the related college subjects that seem the most appealing to you, the most exciting, the most useful, the most revealing, and give some of them a try. There is no reason to embark in advance on some rigid program : let your studies be fluid, play the field as you would play the field of girls before choosing a wife. In both instances, be careful not to give yourself away too soon, body, heart and soul : this is merely the stage of research and investigation. As soon as your choice begins to take shape, concentrate on your " major. " Stick to it long enough to induce new and spiralling interest in it. The more you know about any subject and the more eager you will be to develop this knowledge. Out of hard work, there arises a secondary interest that often has more driving power than the unsubstantial whim that led you to make the choice in the first place.

Ask yourself in what field you can do good—and this does not confine you to corporal works of mercy. It is extremely meritorious and worth-while to feed the poor, heal the sick and bury the dead, but how about trying to put some honesty in advertizing, some substance in television, or some sanity in our relations with China? Have something in mind, and drive towards it relentlessly. Work becomes challenging, exciting, and even easy when we know clearly where we are going, and why : we then have an enormous advantage over the drifters. Choose your field carefully, decide to become an expert in it, and you have a good chance of success.

Be both pliable and wide-awake : you may have started out on the wrong track. As you go along, some other opportunity may open, some entirely new proposition be made to you : study them carefully and check your earlier choices against them. *Follow the spirit wherever it blows, but do not shift with every breeze.* Stick to what you have decided to do, through tiredness and discouragement, through the wear and tear of concentrated, systematic hard work. There is no other formula for true success. You may become rich in many other ways—and poor in many more—but concentrated, intelligent work is the only road to wisdom and creative worth.

It is always wrong to run out on the investment of education and settle for immediate profits. Even if you have to work, beg or borrow, stick it out. The high-school drop-out may be making a fast buck in a garage, but that is probably what he will be doing for the rest of his life.

Aim for an education, not a certificate. The paper itself is worthless if all it proves is that you were there. Kilroy was there, and where did that lead him? Remember that assignments are not impositions to be reduced to the level of minimum pain, but challenges to be raised to that of maximum fruitfulness. If you are not satisfied with the kind of teaching you are getting, speak up clearly and loudly : organize your demands. Lectures should not be sessions of passive boredom. If they are, you are in the wrong classroom and you should get out of it in a hurry. You or your parents are paying for an education, not for adult baby-sitting. You should insist on the right to choose your teachers even if it leads to unbalanced attendance. A good man will be more helpful to a hundred students than a moron to ten—and students have a keen sense of distinction.

Even after you have graduated or completed post-graduate studies, keep on learning. An educated man is one who is aware he knows nothing, and keeps on learning until his last breath. There is always more to be known. Anyone who stops learning is slipping into decay and slow death.

THE CORPORATION MAN AND THE SELF-EMPLOYED

IN MOST of our present educational system, too much importance is given to conformity and too little to the development of personal gifts. Instead of being guided to their individual form of wisdom, children are too often being molded into a pattern of supposed universal acceptance. Everyone needs basic training in the arts of life, but over and above conventional ways, there is an immense area of original endeavor that is all but wasted in the rush for security—the following of conventional tracks that lead to some predetermined slot. The corporation man seems to be favored to the detriment of the creatively self-employed. There are, in fact, a hundred more human and interesting ways of making a living than that of the corporation man, but they all require hard work, imagination and a certain gambling spirit, all of which are rare commodities in a world obsessed with conformism and security.

There are many creative careers in the fields of industrial arts, design, decoration, furniture, photography, illustration, ceramics, plastics, glassware, etc. Then, there is writing, with many diversifications. If anyone had told me, for instance, that there was a mine of both pleasure and profit—not to mention some quite considerable usefulness—in publishing something as highly specialized as a one thousand page Missal in English for Christians of the Oriental Rite, I would have had serious doubts. Yet, the opportunity came and was duly seized at the first knock, and the book is now in print, after years of work, and doing well.

Many people have writing talents without knowing it, but their energy is consumed in routine jobs. Let them hunt for free moments to indulge in their art. Let them try again and again, face mountains of rejection slips : maybe the break will come. The only condition is that they feel in the depth of their souls that they *must* write. If a break does finally come, they may pull out of their uncreative routine progressively and devote more and more time to their writing—until they wake up one morning completely free to do what they are best qualified to do.

Our incorporated world will become less and less tolerable unless there is a tide of revolt against regimentation and conformism, a resurgence of the spirit of creative freedom and originality. There are many new frontiers. Some of them—space exploration, government, education or industry—demand immense organizations and systematic teamwork. Even within them, personal action is possible. Besides these giants, there are many personal niches that are quite original and may be rewarding. Many others are still waiting to be discovered by you. For the man starting at the bottom of an institution, there is very little chance of ever getting to the top. Another, starting on his own, is at the top from the start, and it can be quite exhilarating, if somewhat risky. If things do not seem to work out too well while you are on your own, it will always be time to look for an employer. But at least give yourself a chance as a rising executive in your own chosen field.

It will seldom be possible to visualize the details of a future career. Yet it is quite easy to begin right now the plans of a definite style of life. This will depend upon the proper understanding of what you are, how much you know, and what you want to do with yourself. These three questions coincide with the three main divisions of the present work and with the three attributes of being of scholastic metaphysics : the one, the true and the good. The one " Who am I? " is the object of this first part. The true and the good will be covered in parts II and III.

What you are, the " one " in each person, is a valuable, unique and irreplaceable element in the order of the universe. If you are, it is because you are loved. This will appear more clearly before the end of the book. The fact that you exist is a victory of love, for every human creature is offered a chance to give and receive the bounty of love. The only condition demanded is that he or she say Yes. Yes to himself, yes to others, yes to anything worthy of love that may exist besides or beyond. True life is a quest for love. Everything within the order of right love must be received, everything against it, rejected. The many forms of love must be considered in turn : the well-ordered love of self, including self-respect, self-confidence and the capacity of receiving love; love of neighbor, a sense of shared responsability, a desire to improve the common lot, not through utopian or quixotic reforms, but by simple, discreet, frequent action directed to the immediate welfare of anyone with whom we are related existentially; love of something beyond : the search for the unknown God—but this is the final stage of wisdom, and we shall reach it in due time.

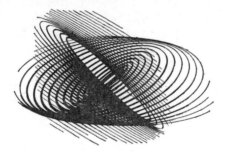

THE NEED FOR STRESS

IN ORDER TO BE EFFECTIVE, a man must have attained a certain dynamic pitch, a certain level of vitality that is sufficient not only to assure his subsistence, but also to provide for outgoing concern. The deepest inner qualities of the human being come out most strongly under conditions demanding the utmost dedication and effort, in times of danger and stress, when there is no more pampering and self-indulgence.

Such conditions are found in war—which also, by a strange economic phenomenon, has been known to rejuvenate an ailing nation. What we need, of course, is not war, but conditions that bring about the same quality of challenge without the elements of destruction and hatred. Such conditions could perhaps be identified with any manner of " frontier" living : that is, with living dangerously, close to nature, at the spearhead of discovery and adventure, in a state of personal engagement so strong and acute that personal survival is at stake. This may be found, not only in the pioneering of land, but in the discovery and exploration of any other frontier of human action : space, medicine, social involvement, or even mystical discoveries.

> Man attains his highest development when he is exposed to the weather, when he is deprived of sleep and then sleeps at length, when his food is alternately abundant and scarce, when he conquers shelter and sustainment through his own effort. He must also exercise his muscles, be tired and rested, fight and suffer, and at times be happy. He must love and hate, his will must be alternately taut and relaxed, he must contend against his equals or himself. He is made for such a manner of existence as the stomach is made to digest food. It is under conditions giving intense play to the processes of adaptation that he becomes more manly. Those who were submitted from childhood to an intelligent discipline, those who have undergone privations and have accomodated themselves to adverse circumstances, are the strong ones, both physically and morally. *

By contrast, when a young man or woman begin life without having had to make the slightest effort to satisfy any need, when not only clothing and shelter and food, but also sports and cars and traveling abroad and any form of pleasure are offered free on a silver platter, all of these things lose much of their incentive as objects of desire. They are so easy to get that they are taken for granted with a total lack of antecedent pleasure and consequent gratitude. The rich child will see a bicycle, ask for it, get it immediately,

* Alexis Carrel, « L'homme, cet inconnu, » Paris, Plon, 1935, p. 294-295. Our translation.

throw it away, and ask for something else. *Nothing is more frustra-ting than the instant gratification of every wish but one—the wish for ALL.*

The same is true on a deeper level of the treasures of sex. *
When casual unions are indulged in at an early age, all the true magic of mutual discovery, all the treasures of expectation, all the joys of offering a well-preserved integrity, disappear in the dreary routine of thoughtless, easy, non-committal bedding.

The decadent loss of manhood and effective action manifested by scions of wealthy families is often due to their self-centeredness, fed to satiety with everything money can buy, never challenged by difficulties or by the need to make an effort of any kind, but gorged instead with sub-human—because excessive—wealth and food and sex.

Drinking and surfing, driving a powerboat or a fast car, party-going and chasing the right kind of girl are all delightful activities in their proper context. But as a way of life, they are totally inadequate and humanly debasing, since man is made for better things. All this is the frosting on the cake, a delightful reward that may be enjoyed after the serious business of living. None of it procures any invol-vement into the core of humanity, into the suffering, anguished, frustrated, oppressed crowd that is crying aloud for help. None of it offers a sufficient outlet to true courage nor to the major virtues of faith, hope and love.

When not properly challenged, the human senses become atro-phied : they lose their tone, their strength and their perceptivity. This is true also of the intellectual and moral powers. People who walk only as far as their car will never know the pleasure of a stroll with a healthful, well-balanced body. Those who never bother to think will lose the power of marveling before the countless wonders of the world. Those who never love will consign themselves to their own private hell.

> How is it possible that a being with such sensitive jewels as the eyes, such enchanted musical instruments as the ears, and such a fabulous arabesque of nerves as the brain can experience itself as anything less than a god? And when

* See *The Virtue of Sex* by José de Vinck, and *The Challenge of Love* by José de Vinck and John T. Catoir listed on page 6 of present book.

you consider that this incalculably subtle organism is insep-
arable from the still more marvelous patterns of its environment—from the minutest electrical designs to the whole
company of the galaxies—how is it conceivable that this
incarnation of all eternity can be bored with being? *

When life is made too easy by the power of wealth, many a
useful challenge is eliminated, many an educational path is made
too smooth and bland. Even food becomes so refined, so soft,
so adulterated as to be insufficient to exercise the functions of
mastication and digestion. Sweetened globs relieve the body of
any functional exertion and it responds by becoming sluggish
and dull.

Stress, then, and effort are conditions of health, well-being and
proper development. By contrast, comfort and laziness are the
shortest roads to extinction of both manliness and feminity. They
reduce life to a languid game in which nothing, not even sex,
procures any fire, liveliness or joy.

Should we then seek some artificial stress? Primitive tribes and
medieval warrior-lords indulged in private wars, seemingly for
no other reason than to keep themselves fit and to strengthen
their breed through the elimination of weaklings. But war is no
longer a relatively harmless pastime for brutes : in our days,
it has reached the unthinkable horror of a H-bomb holocaust,
or drifted into the deplorable smashing of innocents with the most
sophisticated instruments of death in the name of nobody-really-
knows-what. War is no longer popular, except for a few incorrigible
hawks and financial profiteers. And, remember, " War is unhealthy
for children and other living things. "

When unjust and unavoidable war was thrust upon us, there
still was some way of deriving from it some measure of good.
During the brief but violent campaign of the Belgian army in 1940
against Hitler's mechanized hordes, I happened to be with a reserve
unit on the Terneuzen canal, somewhere between Ghent and the
Dutch border. Shells, bombs, small-arms bullets shrieked all around.
A few hundred feet from our machine-gun position, an immense
tank containing some petroleum product was hissing and smoking,
ready to explode and drown us in flames. Black columns of smoke

* Alan Watts, The Book, p. 128

arose from burning towns, forming on the horizon a sinister replica of the Berlin Brandenburg Gate. It is then that I promised that if ever I got out of such a mess, I would never complain about anything.

A few weeks later, after the British debacle at Dunkirk, the Belgian army found itself surrounded, without food, water or ammunition and was forced to choose between useless massacre and surrender; so we ended up as prisoners of the Germans in a camp to the north of Antwerp. We were not mistreated, but deprived of freedom and lacking sufficient water in the hot month of June. I will always remember the day I walked out of that camp, free : the incredible delight of buying a pound of cherries and of being able to go wherever I pleased! Thirty years later, I am still buying cherries and walking around with the same sense of awe.

We appreciate our blessings only when we have been deprived of them. That is where austerity, self-imposed privation, personal discipline have an important part to play. There is nothing more effective than giving up a favorite pastime—be it love-making or anything else—to revive a waning zest for it.

The question, then, is to find out how the pioneer spirit can be maintained and renewed. What needs to be recaptured is the discipline and joy of risk and adventure, the forging into unknown territories through an effort of every power of body and mind, the rising to some worth-while challenge. Let us take a closer look at some of the frontiers opened by modern man.

One of the most obvious is that of space, offering a practical infinity of goals to man's spirit of endeavor. Yet, as it is now being pursued, there is a lack of proportion between the technological triumphs obtained through the spending of immense sums of money, and the crying human needs that are not satisfied because of lack of appropriations. As long as there is that much misery, hatred and ignorance among us, abstract scientific discovery appears as a luxury we cannot yet afford. Of course, the poor will always be with us, but poverty as it exists now could be alleviated considerably with only a small share of the vast amounts spent on trips to the moon, or thrown to the moloch of war.

It is in human relations, human improvements, the meeting of immediate human needs that the new frontiers of our day are to be found. It is there that the most challenging and dangerous battles are being proposed to the courage of our youth disgusted with the profiteering hypocrisy of the many branches of the Establisment. What they will have to face is not bullets, bombs or napalm, but tiredness, misunderstanding, hostility, false accusations by the complacent powers of hyper-conservatism.

The stress-conditions of war that bring out so clearly a strong man's virtues and a weak man's vices are artificial, negative and destructive. The same stress-conditions in the fight for man, the same austerity and dedication, the same occasion for brotherly support and love may be found in the positive and valuable fight against evil, poverty, stupidity and prejudice. To bring out the true values of the young, there is no need for boot-camp—the systematic transformation of a delicate man made for love into an automatic killing-machine. In order to bring out qualities of endurance and courage, there is no need for submission to the degradation of military commands, no need for the brutal physical training.

What every man and woman need as a preparation for a useful and satisfying life is a measure of accepted or even self-imposed austerity. Some forms of hardship must be received and endured, not as ends in themselves, but as a systematic training in view of some higher goal.

To conclude, instead of mollycoddling children and protecting them against every possible discomfort, parents should teach them to rough it : sleep on bare boards from time to time, go without food for a day, suffer hot and cold, camp out, swim in deep lake or moving sea, walk for miles, and discover for themselves the incredible marvel of a glass of water, dry clothing, a bed, the warmth of an open log fire. Parents should provide a rational balance of food and drink, sufficient sleep and exercise, a fitting proportion of work and play, enough fresh air and sunshine, clothing that does not constrict and shoes that do not torture : in a word, a logical and natural adaptation to the world and the weather.

Whenever there is a possibility of choice—and this depends mostly on economic and social circumstances—there is a definite duty to choose the healthier, more natural way of life. When there is no such choice, let us at least do our best to make up for the unnatural conditions of our civilization. If our work consists in sitting all day long behind a desk, recreation—a beautiful word, a meaningful notion—will consist, not in slouching before a TV, or guzzling drinks in a dark and stifling bar, but in getting outdoor for a brisk draught of sunshine, rain or moonlight.

The really vital satisfactions of life come from two sources—from the vitality and meaningfulness of the interpersonal relationships we form; and from the sense of fulfillment we find in creating and producing those things or services which are meaningful to ourselves and others.

LESTER A. KIRKENDALL

Without spiritual insight and generosity, without the ability to rise beyond power and mechanical extensions, man will encounter, in place of the nature which gave him birth, only that vast, expanding genie rising from his own brain—himself.

LOREN EISELEY

The Western mind will have to become quite small again, in order to make room for the supernatural. KARL ADAM

Life has its own natural rhythm which is lacking in a multiplication table; and a prideful progress that tramples life's cadence ends up by killing it with an overload that has no rhythm. RABINDRANATH TAGORE

My freedom and my creative activity are my obedience to the secret will of God. NICHOLAS BERDYAEV

CHAPTER 4

THE PERSON
IN THE STATE OF ACTION

PRODUCTION

OUR PRESENT WORLD and its civilization are based to a high degree on the development of technology. Never in the history of mankind has so much attention been given to the production processes, and never have they yielded such immense returns. Every year, there seems to be a new crop of machines, gadget and accessories of all kinds that quickly assume the character of indispensability, creating both new needs and new jobs.

Yet, the perfecting of processes seems largely limited to material production at the expense of the spiritual and simply human. Things are made by the million. They serve some more or less useful purpose, and they generally work. But where in our days are those masterpieces of quality and refinement that patience and skill alone are able to produce? Where are the truly human treasures of our age? What is being made now is definitely not the humanly good and useful, but the immediately profitable to its maker. A complete change has occurred on the marketplace : instead of needs creating the crafts as in earlier times, it is now the crafts that create the needs, producing such a mass of goods that they must have the costly and artificial boost of advertizing in order to sell.

In many ways, our present life consists in killing ourselves with hard work in order to meet instalments on labor-saving devices we cannot afford and often do not need. Although by now we know *how* to mass-produce, we apply this knowledge in such a way as to rob ourselves of the simple and healthy goods we really need : fresh air, clear water, sunshine, rest, and most of all, love.

Many of our contemporaries seem to be so deeply immersed in the *how* as to have no time left for the *why?* This leads to the multiplication of mad scientists and the opening of Pandora's boxes :

hydrogen bombs, pollution, ecological disasters, overpopulation, economic depressions, wars, etc. People go on and on, producing and working, making more and more gadgets and more and more money, with which they buy more and more of other people's gadgets and cosmetics and soft drinks and artificial pleasure-givers of all kinds that ruin their complexion, their waistline and their zest for life. They seldom have a moment to stop and consider WHY?

There is an urgent need for all of us to enter this world of why, to study religion and philosophy, become acquainted with history and literature and concerned with creative beauty and art. For only then, only after a man or woman of highly specialized skill has been able to integrate this skill in a world where the WHYS have been solved, will his or her castles and bridges and cathedrals and books and power-releasing devices stand as works of wisdom and not as proofs of folly.

Let us not be pessimistic and believe we are doomed : there is still time to act, to guide our world along the ways of truth and sanity by first making ourselves into conscious, creative and loving beings, by taking part in a positive way in the evolutionary *pleroma*—the coming fulfillment of all things in Christ, the Omega Point of Teilhard de Chardin.

UNIVERSAL INTERDEPENDENCE

THERE IS ABOUT US in the universe a pattern of relationship that unites all things into a single unit organically developing under our very eyes. No event can happen anywhere without influencing the whole. As Alan Watts puts it, " you are nothing at all apart from everything else. " This is true even on the lowest level of physical existence and may be witnessed in the law of gravity : every particle of matter seems to act upon every other in order to establish a dynamic equilibrium that tends to repose. Gravitation represents a temporary stage of the interplay of natural forces.

The flight of galaxies is an instance of their imbalance and a sign of the immensity of the order in which they work. Heat and light seem to act in a similar way, diffusing themselves throughout the universe.

In the living world of animals and plants, interdependence appears in that they are subjected to the same universal laws of gravity, light and heat; but also, and characteristically, they are linked by a chain of preceding generations from which they have received what St. Bonaventure calls in medieval terms their " seminal principles, " and which contemporary scientists would describe as genetic traits.

As the world gets smaller because of modern methods of travel and communication, human interdependence becomes more and more obvious. Physically speaking, man, like a stone, a plant or anything else, is dependent upon the universal laws of gravitation, light and heat. As a living being, he has come forth from an immeasurably long chain of ancestors. But while the plant is entirely unconscious and the animal somewhat conscious but not free, man has the privilege of being able to guide his own future by modifying himself and his environment at will. He can, in a sense, create himself and his own world. Not that any man has the power of bringing forth the circumstances of his birth, but that the economic and social conditions of life are the work of man himself, the fruit of freedom used and abused generation after generation. Here, then, is one more link between men : each generation in turn prepares the world into which the next will be born. Our world has been organized, subdivided, industrialized—but also damaged and polluted and complicated and made less and less natural. It is no use complainig or wishing we had been born in a time of greater ease : in fact, the " good old days " are generally seen through a haze, a romantic dream that superimposes upon reality a number of idyllic qualities it never had, and glosses over the immensely heavier burden of hard labor, suffering and early death of the pre-scientific era. We are living now, in this pulsing, breathless, anguished and exhilarating century. In many ways, it is the best that has ever been, and it is the only one we have—two good reasons to make the most of it.

If there seems to be so much tragedy in our present world, it means not that our age is more tragic than others, but that every man's tragedy now becomes our own. When Africans die of hunger, innocents are killed in Asia at the hand of young Americans who also die, when a train crashes in Japan or a dozen school children are crushed by a bus in the US, all these tragedies are flashed to us, and we suffer with their victims, and our hearts long more than ever for peace and love and happiness.

The world is not perfect : it is quite unfinished. At every step, there has to be a fight for justice and order, against the tendency toward chaos that is as much a part of ourselves as it is of our so-called enemies. The greater tragedies of our time are not so much the lost lives as the fact that these same lives are so often wasted, in the wrong places, at the wrong time, and for the wrong reasons, by people of total good will. It was their duty to have known better. In every war, the soldier on each side is offering his life as a sacrifice to human good. He is a martyr of suffering and striving. Too often, alas, he is also the victim of ambitious and greedy men.

Our modern age does give us, better than any other, an opportunity to be responsible, to take part in whatever is going on in the world. Our social responsibility no longer has tribal boundaries : it has taken on global proportions. A civilized man is one who is aware that he is responsible for every man, and feels it, and suffers from the limitation of his power to do something about it—and yet, does what he can within the area of his effective action.

SPORTS AND SERVICES

SPORTS take an important part in recreating modern man. Most of his activities take place in artificial environments, in the polluted athmosphere of a factory or in air-conditioned buildings that do not even have windows in some instances. He is deprived almost entirely of the beneficial effects of ultra-violet and infra-red sunlight, or over-exposed to them. His skin is either bleached or sun-burned, his muscles sag, his general outline resembles that of a pear on two spindles. The desk-dweller is a pale, balding, narrow-shouldered, narrow-chested and heavy-bottomed sitting duck, the natural target for microbes and viruses, neuroses and psychoses, claustrophobia and agoraphobia, allergies, peptic ulcers, throat cancer and heart failure.

At the opposite pole is the professional athlete. Here, everything is sacrificed to performance : health, time, energy, the whole man are given to the single purpose of pushing some ball in a certain way, or improving some existing record. This takes true and harrowing asceticism, but it is inhuman, because what counts in such fake " sport" is not human good, but the feat as an end. The winning champ may end up as a wreck, a cripple or a one-track-minded moron. He may even end up dead, as the roster of murdered boxers and football players so tragically shows. All this effort is devoted to some artificial and non-existing god, some national or local pride, some abstract figure expressed in yards or seconds or runs or goals or what not : the idols are legion. Yet, their commercially cranked-up power holds millions under their sway. There are a few thousand professional performers, and millions of passive fans—the bench-warming " sportsmen" who never practice any sport of their own.

The best of sports, the king of sports—plain walking—has all but disappeared. We ride, we rush, we waddle, we fly. We no longer can afford to mosey along a country lane, since country lanes have disappeared from suburbia where we live. And we ourselves have become numb : who is still able to embark on a voyage of discovery by the simple process of setting down his two feet on a sidewalk and absorbing the marvel, the tragedy and comedy, of any city block?

Nothing procures greater awareness of ourselves and of others than the simple act of walking. The scenery and actors change at a leisurely pace. Faces come close enough for their expressions to be seen—loved or pitied, never scorned, since it is the lack of proximity that occasions scornful pride. To the car driver, the street is filled with nuisances and obstacles, a herd of impersonal impediments to his progress. To the sidewalk pacer, the herd turns into individuals, problems, mysteries, dreams that come and go with the flow of passers-by. And so, the simple, healthy, physical act of walking that had started as a constitutional, turns out to be a means of human contact, of concern and love. There is, for the walker, the deep and rhythmic breathing, the natural balancing of the arms, the stride perhaps consciously smooth, the harmonious motion of

a dance. The very movement keeps the mind alert, on the go, watch-
ful both in self-defense and self-offering. The solicitations of a
changing scenery feed a constant flow of impressions to the senses.
If we are tired or nervous, they may hurt, jangling discordantly,
rattling around in our over-taxed brain. But soon enough the
breathing and the motion, the rhythmic placing of one foot before
the other, the balancing of the body, bring about a physical peace,
an inner silence that at first rejects all noise and recollects itself,
then makes us whole and one—both solitary in the midst of the
crowd and able to share more and more completely some of its
pains and joys.

By contrast, the way of the common variety of modern man—
homo americanus—seems to be one of commotion and un-peace, from
nerve-racking job through nerve-racking traffic, to the nerve-racking
hysteria of spectator sports, and back home to a nerve-racking
evening of violence on TV. No wonder so few people make love
properly : they are totally spent long before their time.

A number of young men, some of them destined to a brilliant
future, have been maimed for life or even killed in a kind of war
game that resembles the initiation practices of primitive tribes,
their fake battles and ritual drawing of blood. The most astonishing
aspect of all this violence is that the reputation of an institute of
higher learning may rise or fall with the success of its team! That
Army and Navy would foster brutal force seems to conform with
their general line of business. But it seems ludicrous to have such
animal spirits sponsored by scholars, sometimes even under the
aegis of the inhabitants of heaven. This may lead to eyebrow-
raising headlines : HOLY GHOST CLOBBERS IMMACULATE
CONCEPTION, or SAINT FRANCIS ROUTS HOLY TRINITY.

As indicated above, some measure of hardship and exertion is
necessary for proper human development. But there is no reason,
except commercial, to make of violence a national pastime. True
sport consists in some pleasantly strenuous activity that enhances
an individual's physical fitness. On the field, the stress is on performance, not on human good. In the bleachers, there is no sport
whatsoever, unless munching, sipping, cheering and yelling,
" Kill the umpire! " may be considered valuable exercise. The
regular sports fan is as well developed as Simon Stylite : there is
not much difference, physically speaking, between spending a
lifetime on a column or on a bench.

Could no better use be found for this enormous energy, hard work, time, space and money; for all the intelligence and human resources wasted on the practice and observation of activities that seem totally unrelated to the realities of human life? The Romans had *panem et circenses*—bread and the circus—and history tells where it led them. We now have hot dogs and the ball games.

This is one more point where the younger generation should take over. There are several possible remedies. One consists in activities outside of sport that are really useful, personally and socially; another, in practicing rational, human, participator sports in a moderate way.

After World War II, several groups of young people from Belgium and France went about Germany rebuilding with their own hands the churches that had been destroyed by bombing. All they asked for were the materials and frugal bed and board. At first, they encountered suspicion, but as soon as their intentions were understood, they were very well received. In return, a group of German students built the church of the Reunion at the Protestant Monastery of Taizé in France.

In every country, there is available and enormous reservoir of energy and good will that is waiting to be tapped and organized. What is needed is inspiration, leadership, a catalyst that could transform latent energy and good will into action. The " lost generation" is a myth. Beatnicks and hippies are not lost : they may be confused, but they are positively seeking a better way. The greatest majority of the youth of our time is ready, eager and willing to contribute to this better way, and their idealism is being challenged by such organizations as the Peace Corps, and several private groups such as the Grail, the Papal Volunteers, the Catholic Workers and the Madonna House Lay Apostolate in Combermere, Ontario, Canada.

The question of a two-year social service as an alternative to military service should be considered very seriously. The system has a number of advantages and disadvantages. On the one hand, it will no longer let about half the male population contribute no service at all while the other half is serving heavily. On the other it will be hard to find useful means of employment for the untrained, the unbalanced, the unwilling.

CREATIVITY

IN ORDER TO REMAIN alert and alive, we need something to look forward to. Were it not for hope, life on earth would be intolerable. Tiring or dreary work is possible only because the siren will blow at the end of the day, saturday will come at the end of the week, and vacation time at the end of the year. A lifetime of work will be geared to retirement, and life itself, to the expectation of heaven.

But this is true only of sub-human, joyless and uncreative work, in which there is no progress, no fulfillment, no foreseeable time when something great and good will have been achieved. Ideal work consists in the maturing of one's original thought, its elaboration through slow and often painful processes, its growth and progress and final flowering into something really new or beautiful or good. Such are the jobs of the writer, the scientist, the artist, the priest, and also of others in the fields of teaching and health.

The virtue of hope keeps us going : hope in a better world, improved social or financial conditions, for ourselves, our families and others; hope for more freedom and time to enjoy the glories of life, and greater opportunities to help and give. The logic of persevering work is that it tends to some definite goal : something to look forward to. There is no reason why a worth-while goal could not be combined with some healthy stress, right here and now. Let us set our aim high even if it takes discipline, hardship and sacrifice. Why not try, for instance, for a post-graduate degree, the mastering of a foreign language, or some specialized skill such as drawing, dancing, or playing some musical intrument? All of these require considerable effort, but are highly rewarding.

The more educated we become, the greater will be our human worth. Truly great artists or specialists in any field, men and women deservedly at the top of their profession, are often humble, simple, unassuming people because they have no need to throw their weight around to prove how great they are : they themselves stand as proofs of their success. Arrogant and pretentious people have not truly arrived, nor are they truly great : they are trying to prove how superior they are, while at the same time offering evidence of their failure.

A truly creative mind appears as a miracle to those who enjoy the productions of intelligence while lacking the ability to bring them into being. A creative artist, architect, writer, scientist or engineer seems able to snatch some kind of completed form out of thin air. The product of his skill seems to come fully armed, as Athena from the brow of Zeus. There is no visible process of creation : a thing of truth or beauty seems to come suddenly into being without any labor or parentage.

Actually, what is visible is but the flowering of a long, painful and often discouraging process. Each blossom of creativity is the topmost shoot of an elaborate growth that comprises the roots of obscure beginnings, endless attempts and failures, false starts and disappointments, but most of all, an unbroken chain of single-minded, persevering efforts toward a clearly intended goal.

Creativity is the result of the systematic training of perfectibility. Every one of us is born with a malleable, receptive, indefinitely trainable intelligence. What we do with it depends upon our own free choice. In most instances, there is little preplanning, for the hardships and necessities of daily survival may absorb almost all our energies. As soon as we have reached a sufficient level of freedom and leisure, as soon as our civilization can afford to do more than barely survive, there comes the possibility of organized culture, of directed development. To put this in simple language, as soon as we are safely housed, clothed and fed, we can give some attention to what we are going to do.

To conclude : creative intuition has something gratuitous, some quality of lightning. It does not come, however, to the unprepared mind. What seems to be an entirely spontaneous and free process is in fact the result of the rational power working through the fantastic network of nerves in the brain. In order to have valid intuitions, the mind needs to be richly nourished with experience and truth, that is, with the materials to be combined, and the principles of their orderly arrangement. No flash of discovery every rises from a blank and slovenly intellect. All the elements of a problem must be present before any solution can be worked out. When it does appear, it seems to have the gratuitous and enchanting freshness of creation because the links of the chain of reasoning that made it rise are lost in the unconscious mind.

PART II

THE PHILOSOPHICAL PROBLEM
OF PERSONAL LIFE

What is Truth?

There are five cycles, Ego, Humanity, Earth, the Universe, God. I describe how we ascend all these steps, and when we reach the highest, how we live simultaneously all the previous cycles. NIKOS KAZANTZAKIS

Order gives way to new order—in an orderly way, but not entirely orderly, that is, not without the unpredictable play of history, of space and time. RAYMOND J. NOGAR

The individual may be said to recapitulate aspects of the human history in his intellectual and spiritual development. JOHN R. SILBER

We live in several worlds, each one more real than the one within; and in relation to the one that overlaps it, each world fails. CLAUDE LEVI-STRAUSS

Only a man who has a firm grasp of the over-all picture of life and existence can use the individual sciences without harming himself. FRIEDRICH NIETZSCHE.

CHAPTER 1

THE CONCENTRIC
CYCLES OF TRUTH

CYCLES SEEN AS FRAMEWORKS

IN ORDER TO FUNCTION PROPERLY, the mind needs a framework, a certain number of points of reference in relation to which action may be organized. This is true of the very beginning of conscious life both in the child and in the human race, and of the loftiest systems of theology and philosophy. The necessity of a framework, a certain " cycle" of truth, extends from the dawn of mankind to the atomic age, from pre-kindergarten to Teilhard de Chardin, and beyond.

The first cycle is that of the unborn child confined to the warmth of the womb. Then comes the initial breaking of a cycle, the violence of birth, the gasp for air and the sudden cry. Very soon, this new cycle is enlarged in turn to include sight and hearing, the presence of people and things, the familiar surroundings of crib and room. These are the child's gods : food and air and touch and hearing and sight, these all-powerful necessities of early life. They contain him, encircle him, marking the boundaries of his reach, of the things that act upon him and upon which he in turn can act.

With further growth, the cycle breaks again to expand once more. Its radius extends to include the house, then grows larger and larger with each new break to encompass the neighborhood, the city, the country, the world, the whole universe—even the possibility of other worlds and other universes, and finally, that of other orders of being.

At each of these stages, there is a corresponding cycle of knowledge that includes the preceding ones, but also implies a break away from them into some greater dimension of thought, expressed through a specific philosophy, acting through specific rules, and worshiping a specific set of gods. These serve as pegs, or formal certainties without which there can be no accumulation of learning, no building of a consistent whole for lack of a solid frame. In the absence of these gods and of contact with them, there is nothing but the closed world of the subjective mind.

The course of human life may be seen as the passing from one framework to the next through a successive breaking of the concentric cycles of knowledge. Each step from one cycle into the next is in a sense a denial, or rather, a surpassing of the preceding one. Progress will always consist in crossing a certain number of threshholds, which entails each time some kind of risk, a crisis, a plunging into the unknown : birth, the awakening of conscious life, leaving for school, adolescence, marriage, and death : the final jump into the totally unexplored.

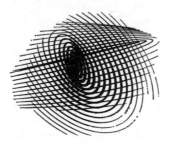

THREE CONTEMPORARY ATTITUDES

THE PRESENT anguish and upheavel in the Catholic Church may be seen as the passing from the cycle of passive and confident absolutism, an adolescent state, into that of responsible adulthood. It is well expressed by Andrew Greeley : " The principal reason for the low morale in certain sectors of the Church today is that the post-Vatican Council revolution has forced large numbers of people to face the God question who were shielded from it by the rigid authoritarian structure of the old Church. " *

* National Catholic Reporter, April 1, 1970.

Humanity has developed along the same lines as the individual. It has known a period of infancy in the proper sense of the word : a time when there was no speech. It has known a period of limitation to the immediate concerns of daily survival, a childhood during which every unexplained power was believed to be a god. It has gone through the awakening of rational thought—and many other stages leading to the present human condition of both awareness and anguish.

All men do not coincide in terms of development with the higher specimens of their age. There are many cases of stunted growth, of individuals fixed on the mental or emotional level of an earlier stage. * Some have remained behind because of the insufficiency of their mental endowment, others because of insufficient or defective education. What we are concerned with here is the cycle of thought developed by leaders in the fields of psychology, philosophy and theology.

Three different attitudes seem to be courting the mind of civilized Western man : the *conservative-dogmatic*, the *nihilistic-existential*, and the *progressive-problematical*.

On the conservative-dogmatic side are all those whose classical culture resulted in deep respect for the past. They are aware of the wealth and power of human thought; they have assimilated a closed system of refined and elaborate teachings, the rich fruits of many thinking generations. This, they say, is the Wisdom of the Ages, the *philosophia perennis*. Most of these men are scholars and supporters of Church institutions. Their major task is the preservation of treasures. Their good faith is generally impeccable and their erudition profound. But they tend to look with suspicion upon any innovation, any departure from classical forms, any adventure in the rich and tempting fields of the new theology or philosophy. For such men as these, all has been said and well said, and nothing remains to be done but to perpetuate acquired wisdom and teach it to those who seek the one and only truth.

What is right with such a system is that it defends a valuable framework, one that has well-established and accepted points of reference. What is wrong with it is that, instead of seeing *any* system for what it is—precisely a system, and nothing more, one of

* See Charles A. Reich, " The Greening of America" for a description of three distinct stages of development in the United States, which he calls consciousness I, II and III.

the grills upon which the mind can store and organize its scattered experience—it tends to see and promote itself as if it were the final and unalterable explanation of all things, the ultimate cycle of wisdom, instead of one of the concentric cycles. It has allowed its postulates and frames of reference to harden into absolutes. *

Such is the prevailing attitude in conservative institutions, universities and seminaries, in Rome and elsewhere. Strangely enough, the Marxist philosophies are to be included in this same conservative-dogmatic category. There is nothing progressive or problematical about them : there is no place in them for doubt or dissent. Their position is even more triumphalistic than that of the most backward member of the Curia—although for entirely different reasons.

For the conservative-dogmatic theologian, there are no problems. There may still be mysteries, but even these are carefully analyzed and defined, sometimes even " solved " through nominalistic verbiage, in the style of Molière's doctor who explained gravely that the reason why a certain drug put people to sleep was its " soporific virtue. " ** Final answers can then be given to every question, rational or moral, so that life is made to appear as a well-defined and completely foreseeable set of events through which man can navigate safely by the simple means of following the Rules of the Establishment. No churchman in authority ever seems to have said, " I don't know. " The irreality and impracticality of such an attitude is perhaps the reason for Pope Paul's anguish and embarrassment in the Birth Control debate.

Life and reality are neither foreseeable nor analyzable in full. As whe have seen, they are fluid, dynamic, unexpected, inexhaustively surprising and different, so unpredictable in their variety that no institution could ever promulgate rules fast enough to cope with their ongoing rush. Every man and every woman are unique at every moment of their life. Every life is personal and essentially impenetrable. Every instant within every life is a one-of-a-kind experience related in a unique and inexplicable way to the whole universe. It has never happened before and will never happen again.

Wherever we look, we can witness, not the formal and logical growth of well-organized rational beings developing according to

* See pp. 139 ff. where this notion is developed.
** " Le médecin malgré lui "

plan, but a clumsy, maddening, frustrating series of thrusts, attempts,
gropings by individual members of the human family; a rocking motion
from genius to insanity, with no clear distinction in between; a jumble
of lusts and depravities vying with holiness and heroism under the
thin coat of conventional restraint enforced by public and religious
authorities.

The plan—supposing there is one—exists, not on the level of
the individual here and now, but on that of immense numbers
throughout the ages. For each individual observer, the vision is
fragmentary : he can perceive at any one time but a small area of
life, witness the capers of but a few of his fellow-men. Such a close-
range vision may lead to belief in the absurdity of it all, and so
we are now faced with another major philosophy of life : nihilistic
existentialism.

For Jean-Paul Sartre and his followers, the *nihilistic existentialists*,
everything is absurd, for they live within the boundaries of their
own closed-in absurdity. Having no vision of any form of existence
beyond absurdity, they are forced to remain prisoners of their
own absurd existence. A man who wishes to prove to himself that
all men are absurd by consorting with none but absurd men may
have made a subjective point to his own satisfaction—or despair.
But he cannot profess the absurdity of the universe without falling
into the old fallacy of taking the particular for the universal. If
the nauseated Jean-Paul Sartre insists on seeing nothing but the
nauseating, that is his business, but he cannot extend his doctrine
to anybody else. People who start from the premise that nothing
makes sense have no logical basis for indoctrinating others.

And so, nihilistic existentialism suffers in its self-made hell.
" *L'enfer, c'est l'autre.* " " Hell is the other guy—or gal. " The
Sartrean first principle seems to be, " Hate your neighbor as your-
self, and relish the emotional impact of this self-inflicted torture. "
This is an expression of the death-wish, the exact counterpart
of the word of life, " Love your neighbor as yourself. "

Of course, there is here much of the over-dramatization dear
to the French heart : the exaggeration of self-induced complication
and of the consequent suffering. The amazing thing, however, is that
such a masochistic approach received so wide a response in the
intellectual world when the only sane reaction would have been a
burst of Homeric laughter. For survival is impossible without a
sense of humor, as it is impossible in a world that makes no sense.

Everyone must have his reason to live, otherwise he will remove himself from among the living.

There is another form of existentialism, the *progressive-problematical*. It explodes once and for all the lulling myth : " God's in his heaven, all's well with the world!" The only way out of such foolish complacency—and of the mess of despair—will consist in taking life as it is, with its imperfections, miseries and disappointments, but also with its moments of blinding joy and the many dew-drops of its minor pleasures : to take life and say YES to it, as we shall see, not in spite of everything, but because of everything : because of that larger vision that will let us see beyond the bickering of men, beyond even their staggering stupidity, pride, shortsightedness and fear of each other that have so often led to war and may one day result in the destruction of us all; because of the ability to see beyond all this, to hear beyond the weeping and groaning of hungry, frustrated, desperate crowds another voice, " for see, the winter is past, the rains are over and gone. The flowers appear on the earth, the time of pruning of vines has come, and the song of the dove is heard in our land." (Cant., 2 : 11-12).

Perhaps we may see in this the perfect creed of the true flower-children, of those who seek to live through love and to " prune the vine" of society of its many abuses. Indeed, may the song of the dove be heard in our land, but we will all have to work hard to make it come about.

There is, then, in the progressive-problematical attitude a very real and actual understanding of the importance of human effort, human intelligence, human suffering and toil. Man is seen no longer as a puppet at the mercy of some external Providence or deterministic nature, but as realizing the god-in-him through a series of " agonizing reappraisals," that is, readjustments to what is encountered in the successive cycles of reality, reassessments of the meaning of truth and life and love.

Such a reassessment is a matter of art, of eliminating non-essentials in order to adapt oneself to the very core of what actually is. Contemporary art, for instance, is doing away with the conventions of classicism in that it tends no longer to imitate nature, but to express man. Its ways are at times senseless, but they are genuinely valid when spontaneous and originally human. Likewise, contemporary philosophy, instead of concentrating on minute details, should attempt to offer a better image of the whole human complex. *

THE HIGHEST CYCLE OF WISDOM

NO LONGER do we have a model set before us, a complete and static wax figure with which we can identify in complete security : most of our present-day experiences are so new that we need a spirit of exploration to deal with them properly. Does this mean that every old concept should be thrown out, that classical philosophy is invalid and that we should start all over again from scratch? Not in the least. The iconoclast, one who would do away with every representation and image under the pretext that none is fully adequate, may be seen as a waster of ancient wisdom.

The different cycles of knowledge are not mutually exclusive : they are concentric. The security of the smallest, the womb, was true and good. The warm crib enlarged it without destroying its original value, but on the contrary, adding further dimensions. The home, the neighborhood, the city, the country, the world and the universe continued the expansion : they completed each other without eliminating completely the preceding stage.

* An editorial in the July 27, 1970, Issue of *Publisher's Weekly*, is significative in this regard. It discusses the future of University presses and other scholarly publishers and concludes as follows : " Interdisciplinary books, really generic books are what is needed if academic publishers—whether affiliated with a university or not—are going to maintain their relevance.... The seminal work is replacing the specialized monograph."

Many disciplines of thought seem to be progressing along the same road—from one cycle to another, from one theory to the next, each one providing an additional clue. See for instance the development of quantum mechanics, from the views of Bohr to present interpretations. And the same goes for theology and philosophy. All was not wrong with a theology that deified the sun, the earth, fire or the process of propagation of life : such things are properly divine, by reflection and in the form of signs, but also in their origin and purpose. But the truly divine is greater than them all. Nor is it heretical to revere science, the discoveries of the inner working of matter or of the human body, for that too is divine—and yet the divine is greater than any science. Nor again is it wrong to greet with respectful devotion the monuments of human thought : the great systems of philosophy, the deistic or atheistic attempts to explain all things by confining the universe within the mesh of a logical reference pattern. But supreme reality—the divine—once again is too great to be contained in any one system, since it is essentially uncontainable, being ALL, and therefore infinitely remote from *any* system.

And so, it is perfectly possible, in fact, it is fitting and right, to see the philosophies and theologies of established Churches, not as final and absolute stages of human knowledge, but as the temporary result of concentric cycles of growth, and to look beyond them in order to be free of some of their all-too-human prejudices and limitations.

But does this attitude of freedom not throw us back into the isolation of the primitive, or into that subjective double-talk that may mean one thing to the speaker and another to the listener? Not if we work with our neighbors, through parallel efforts. There is in the mind a natural soundness, a series of open paths that may lead progressively to maturity and development when properly followed. There are also means of communication, a bell that rings when two minds in unison strike a common note and greet each other through intellectual assent. We are definitely not alone. But the trouble is that, at every climb, there is the possibility of a false step, a misinterpretation, an exaggerated attention to some secondary way, and also, I suspect, a number of different and yet legitimate paths to the top. Add to these difficulties the blind opposition of people left below, and you will have a glimpse of the dangers of creative intellectual life.

What we are seeking are the spontaneous and gratuitous experiences of life. Such flowers do not grow in thin air : they need a stem to support them, roots to feed them, leaves to transform solar energy into assimilable substance. The rich humus in which life grows is made of decaying remnants of earlier forms of life. *Flowers grow, not from the destruction of other lives, but through their sacrificial transformation into materials of life.*

In the same sense, no new theology or philosophy can be created *ex nihilo*. Everything we do well is founded on experience, on the rich soil of other generations, other lives, other loves.

What if those who came before us were primitive, unsuccessful, ridiculous even in our sophisticated eyes? Without them, we would not have come to life. They too may have had our dreams, and tried but they lacked our chances of success. It is not by living meticulously by the standards of the past that we shall succeed, nor is it by rejecting them totally, but by developing, unfolding, revealing what had existed all along, as yet unborn and unseen. We must produce out of the past, out of earlier experience and experimentation, and not reject them as a whole.

At this point, the necessity of serious study becomes obvious. If we are to take advantage of earlier discoveries, we must go back to former times, consider their methods, their successes and failures, and carry on from there. Quite often, it will be enough to get rid of gingerbread and furbelows to discover a sound structure—and it is much less wasteful to do so than to start building a new house. Few of us have the genius and the energy to build. Many of those who tried have cheated on the foundations and their philosophical or theological structures crumbled into oblivion.

Study, read, investigate, question experts long before you begin to build anything of importance—and twice as much before you begin to destroy. The image of your dream-house, of your dream-world, will make logical, structural, effective sense only after you have had a good look at the house that Jack built. Your examination should be neither superficial nor supercilious, so that even if Jack made a mess of it, he will have helped you avoid the same mistakes.

And so it is with wisdom in theology and philosophy. There is such a thing as the Wisdom of the Ages : it is contained in the Great Books, the Bible, Plato, Aristotle, Bonaventure, Thomas Aquinas, Dante, Shakespeare, and scattered throughout the works of more recent thinkers. It is a great pleasure to go treasure-hunting through them in search of gems of truth, and a delight to discover them. And the more unexpected the place of finding, the greater the pleasure because of the effect of surprise. But together with the spirit of *recovery* that corresponds to archeological diggings, there is the much more exciting experience of *discovery*, of your own advancing one step further in the art of making new things out of old and even, for the intellectual and artistic creator, out of new.

The world is various, of infinite iridescent aspect, and until I attain to a corresponding infinite variety of statements, I remain far from anything that could in any sense be described as " truth. "   HAVELOCK ELLIS

There are more things in heaven and earth, Horatio, than are dreamt of in your philosophy.   WILLIAM SHAKESPEARE

That which you know fills you. That which you do not know fills the universe.   VLADIMIR GHIKA

Reality is not necessarily clear and simple. We cannot even be certain it is always within our grasp.   ALEXIS CARREL

Truth is not something that can be learned once and for all and then simply repeated. Truth means lovingly accepting the will of God from moment to moment and carrying it out.   HANS URS VON BALTHASAR

Truth is not the adequacy of our representative operations, but the adequacy of our conscious existence. More precisely, it is the fidelity of consciousness to being…. Truth can be understood as an existential relation of self to being which must by definition develop in order to realize itself—and not as a relation of conformity to an objective thing which must by definition be stable in order to be at all.   LESLIE DEWART

Life is always an exception, a statistical random phenomenon.   CARL JUNG

In all important matters, we work for the uncertain.   BLAISE PASCAL

CHAPTER 2

HUMAN TRUTH :
IMPERFECTION

CONTEMPORARY PHILOSOPHY

WE ARE ALL SEEKING THE TRUTH, but what is it? And where is it to be found? Is truth a matter of mental inebriation, a vision brought about by a prophetic spirit or released by some potion or drug? Is truth a subjective state, or is it objective? Is truth in us or in the world? Do we have to wait until it comes to us, or chase it and hound it from now to eternity, from here to the remotest galaxy? Is truth the same for you and me—and a few billion other human beings? Is there such a thing as truth, anyway, or is it a mere dream of the mind? Is there such a thing as a dream? And is there a mind?

Philosophies come and go with the contradictions and absurdities of a Mad Hatter's Tea Party. They mix and coalesce and intertwine, leaving a nightmarish jumble of thoughts and principles that fight for predominance in daily life. Many fade into oblivion. Others harden and become absolute dictates, acting as the motors of a given society. They are often little more than a collection of prejudices brought to the fore by some strong personality that has distilled them from a mass of ambient tendencies. They often assume reassuring names : freedom, democracy, republicanism, human dignity. What, in fact, do they amount to? Freedom from opposition—but also freedom to oppress. Democracy as long as it helps those in power—but autocratic dictatorship as soon as they can get away with it. Republicanism in principle a search for the " common thing, " the " common good "—automatically identified with the good of the ruling clique. The dignity of our own person soon taken as the indignity of everyone else, particularly if they happen to be different, and unforgivably, if they happen to be superior. In the name of freedom, of liberalism, millions of workers become slaves in the nineteenth century; in the name of communism, the common good, other millions are oppressed; in the name of the dignity of the race, eight million Jews are murdered.

A Frenchman once defined memory as the faculty that forgets. Likewise, intelligence could be defined as the faculty that makes mistakes, and the will, as that which chooses wrong. Does this mean there is no hope for truth? Let us try to get more deeply into the understanding of truth as related to philosophy, and of philosophy as related to practical wisdom.

Philosophy, etymologically speaking, is the love of wisdom and its object is the search for truth. Wisdom is the art of happiness, and truth is the way to it.

In our days, however, philosophy seems to have assumed a different meaning : it generally refers to the art of talking about words and thinking about thoughts, a kind of intellectual juggling in which the mind analyzes and admires its own subtlety for the sake of its own pleasure, and that of other subtle minds. The purpose of contemporary philosophy does not seem to be the happiness of living man, but the dazzling of a few specialized scholars able to make sense out of the tricks and fireworks of other scholars. Philosophy has become the esoteric exercise of a single function—analysis—considered independently of its action on man.

Take for instance a highly fashionable discipline, symbolic logic. Symbolic logic is a tool of reasoning. It amounts to a quasi-mathematical formulation of deduction. Its order is purely abstract. It is both universal in its application and independent from any actual content of thought. Its truth exists within itself, unaffected by the truth or falsity of its premises. This indicates both its strength and its weakness.

The strength of symbolic logic is that it constitutes a valid system that works in any time, language or content as does mathematics. Its weakness is that, as a tool, it is useful only when applied to reality. In itself, it is a kind of game that may be of interest to the specialist, as abstract calculation is of interest to the mathematician. But it has very little to do with reality. As Nicholas Berdyaev put it so well, " logistic empiricists of our time attempt to replace metaphysical problems with logical and purely formal tricks. "

Considered in relation to philosophy as a whole, symbolic logic plays an extremely small part. A perfect symbolic logician may be at the same time the most unwise and unhappy man on earth. The weakness of the system is the same as that of abstract deductive reasoning itself : its validity, intrinsically perfect, may be completely voided by false assumptions contained in the premises to which it is applied. As long as it remains in the abstract, confined to its own symbols, it is both absolutely true and completely sterile. As soon as symbols are replaced by concepts, reasoning becomes potentially fruitful, but also liable to error because of the impossibility of perfect conceptual definition. Symbolic logic would have profound importance only if each symbol could be replaced by a word, and each word by a concept identically understood by every mind. What happens, in fact, is that any word in any language may represent a number of different concepts, and every concept may have a different interpretation in each mind, so that speech is never univocal, but only analogical. We never speak " of" the same thing, but" about" the same thing. Hence, applying symbolic logic to analogical terms necessarily destroys its certainty and perfection.

When we speak with another man, we never know with absolute clarity what we are talking about, we never find the exactly right words to express it, our listener never gets the exactly intended meaning out of the words we use, and he has his own interpretation of the concepts they represent. A conversation, then, is little more than a hit-and-miss attempt at exchanging approximate notions between two people who do not quite know what they are talking about. The marvel is that it makes any sense at all!

The erroneous belief in the absolute practical value of symbolic logic is not a modern phenomenon : one of the major errors of medieval philosophy was to have imprudently built a system of thought on the premise of the absolute content of terms and concepts, and to have drawn from it whole structures of absolute conclusions.

The main value of symbolic logic, then, is not to procure truth, but to eliminate gross errors by pointing out those forms of reasoning that are intrinsically invalid, that is, invalid in any case, independently of the terms substituted for the symbols. This is not going very far on the way to wisdom, but it is one short step. Mathematics alone is truly logical, and the reason is that it depends upon no-thing : it is built on quantity alone, a simple, abstract notion characteristic of all material objects, due to their attribute of spatio-temporality. Any attempt at extrapolating mathematical

logic and making it apply to things is doomed to failure, because
no things can be known with that degree of evidence represented
by the notion of quantity and its derivatives.

For philosophical logic to be an exact and scientific method, it
would have to imply a perfect understanding of all the terms
involved in a reasoning. The fact is, however, that no human being
has any such understanding about anything. He does not even
know with a reasonable amount of accuracy either what or who he
is. He has only vague notions about his own person, soul, thought,
life, ego. He is constantly surprised and upset by the resurgence
of inner forces he can hardly control. In fact, he is almost a stranger
to himself.

If man can hardly know his own self, if his intelligence is unable
to conceive clearly the very being of which it is the light, how
can he claim to know other intelligences, other persons? He has
with them fleeting, superficial, sensory contacts that need to be
processed by fantastically complicated mechanisms in order to
become conscious thoughts. Some of these thoughts do correspond to
a certain degree with what their object is : man is able to obtain
some objective information and to establish some subjective contact
in regard to other men. But such an imperfect relationship cannot
serve as the basis for any absolute judgment.

The same is true, not only of other people, but also of any other
thing, be it the whole universe or the simplest atom : we as men
simply do not know what they are and cannot afford to use any of
them as the terms of some absolute reasoning. This was understood
in part by the ancients whose logic was based, not on individual
people or things, but on the " universals "—abstract notions
corresponding to some common characteristic present in a given
group of beings. But the very notion of an universal is based on
another, prior idea : the absolute static immutability and mutual
irreductibility of essences. The thought was that things were what
they were, once and for all; that animal could not become man, nor
man evolve, that all species were absolutely distinct and separate, etc. If abstract and fixed essences existed as such, as Plato
believed, then there would have been a rational basis for absolute
logic. What is correctly said of man at one time would then always
and everywhere apply to him, for the term man would refer to a
number of notes clearly understood and expressed in the simplest
definition, using genus and specific differences : man is of the genus

animal, the specific difference being rationality. On such a basis, absolute logic and absolute morality would have been valid. But let us take an existential look at this apparently marvelous system. Unfortunately, man-as-such does not exist, for all that ever existed and will ever exist are individual men—and to make things even more complicated, every one of them is changing constantly.

PHILOSOPHY OF THE INDIVIDUAL

HOW DOES an individual come to be what he or she is? There is a twofold problem of origin : that of the species and that of the person. In the traditional religious system developed by Scholasticism, man originated fully rational and complete from the creative act of God. Since his earliest origin, he enjoyed the full power of rational thought and was able to perform meritorious or sinful acts according as he conformed to his nature or contradicted it. The person came to be at the instant of conception, at which time the child received from God (Creationism) and not from his parents (Traducianism) a complete rational soul, enjoying from this moment the full rights of a human being. With the discoveries of evolution and the development of an existential and dynamic philosophy of man, there is now serious doubt as to the accuracy of this simple and even simplistic view.

Existentially speaking, truth is practical. It corresponds, not to what things are imagined to be (rationalism), but to what they actually are (realism). A man on earth is true to himself in the measure in which he lives intensely and loves with art and ardor whatever is worthy of his love. The intensity of life is a matter of eagerness, concern, healthy and avid curiosity that seeks personal fulfillment and discovers soon that it is attainable only through others. *The truth of life, then, is not a matter of self-perfection, nor a lonely road to personal salvation, but a headlong plunge into the turmoil of complex reality, a loss of selfishness in the seething ocean of the joys and sorrows, births and deaths, victories and defeats of the mass of humanity struggling toward its final and complete fulfillment.*

We are constantly ascending toward our own truth, or falling away from it. Not one instant of our conscious life is neutral or unimportant. Even our sleep may be helpful or destructive, for it may be a means for restoring us either to ascent or to descent. And not a single instant of our time will ever return to be repaired, healed or enjoyed once more. (" I once tried to recapture a moment like this... Dio mio, che disastro!" says Fellini in " The Mirror of Venus, " speaking of a moment of love.) We are in the midst of the constant flow of a one-way traffic, incessantly building or ruining ourselves. Every moment has its personal challenge that I alone can meet. Every chance given to me is unique and of infinite weight, for my everlasting destiny will depend upon the sum of them all.

Existential knowledge—the logic of man—is the understanding of things as they really are. It is true in the measure in which what the mind possesses corresponds to some objective reality. One of the first questions, then, will be : does anything exist outside of the mind? Is all of the world around us a ploy created by our own imagination? Is it all a projection of our dreams, a construction of phantoms and phantasms, that fit our own desires? If this were true, our dream-world would coincide with the goal of these desires : total order and harmony resulting in total happiness, in a non-frustrated and eternally renewed activity of love. But clear proof that the world is no subjective creation may be found in the objective evidence of suffering. The outside world intrudes brutally into our private paradise, replacing a hoped-for perfection with an all-too-real imperfection before which mind and will and the freedom of both are forced to bow.

Another proof of the objectivity of the world around us is the fact that the experience of suffering is shared by all men, time and time again, following the same patterns in every destiny. Since the world makes us suffer in countless ways, and also procures an infinity of unexpected and unplanned pleasures, it proves itself objective, external to our minds. In a word, as pain is proof of the world's objectivity, so also is pleasure : the flash of delight, the surprising and gratuitous contact with the true, the good and the beautiful.

Other philosophers have claimed that, although we do not create our world, we are one within its universal spirit, thus participating in a single world-soul as a substantial although imperfect fragment. This notion leads to the denial of the individual personality, of the real distinction between separate thinking, living and loving beings. It makes of the sum of human spirits the reason and the end of the universe. Since the sum of imperfect spirits can produce nothing more than an imperfect whole, the notion of a world-soul does not satisfy our craving for the all-perfect Reality. In order to survive rationally, we need, if not the certainty, at least the hope of effective action upon ourselves and our surroundings, leading to an eventual fulfillment of our highest desires. Autistic children become so because of some early experience in frustration through lack of response : they were often so badly neglected that their cries for help and their appeals for love failed to bring about the expected and much-needed answers. Believing themselves unable to communicate effectively, they cease to communicate at all.

In order, then, to establish normal human relations, communication is a must. It consists essentially in the two-way traffic of receiving true information and affection and transmitting them effectively. The first step of communication will be the acquiring of knowledge—the reception and storage of communicable material.

The acquiring of human knowledge is little more than a form of groping : it is a long and tedious hit-and-miss procedure that has been going on since the very beginning of conscious thought. It consists essentially in the transmission from generation to generation of a core of information—and misinformation—that needs to be relearned, reassimilated, reappraised and reformulated by every mind that develops from childhood to maturity. The sum-total of human knowledge has now attained such a staggering volume that no single human brain could contain it. The most that any modern man can learn is some general view of the whole, with perhaps a deeper insight into some particular area of discovery.

Many people never go to the trouble of learning at all : they are content with receiving, storing or discarding random impressions as they come. Even when they do make an effort of formal, organized learning, few people really succeed in assimilating properly the data of the past. Fewer still can appraise such data in a way that leads to progress. *The unlearned live by blind conformity; the non-assimilating, by borrowed rules of thumb; the uncritical, by prejudice. Only those who enjoy a cultured analytical and integrated mind have a chance to live as free creative spirits in the midst of a world of mass culture that is no culture at all.*

There is a great difference between a healthy hunger for knowledge and the prideful search for absolute certainty in all domains. " Eat of this and you will be gods. " Swallow the technology of the modern world, and you will have the answer to everything. Study Aquinas to the last comma, and you will be able to face every moral and theological question with a final and absolute answer. What a pitiful and yet widespread folly! As if any single discipline could contain the answers to every possible question of life!

At the beginning of the search for knowledge and truth, there is then the need to order and sort the possibilities, to hierarchize values in relation to a logical scale that will attribute to each level of investigation the precise importance it deserves. An intelligent man needs such a scale as a reference to help him determine the better choice at every crossing or dividing of the way. The first step, then, is to find out what *is* important, what is worth long days and nights of study, the sacrifice of leisure and pleasure. By contrast, in the *carpe diem, dolce vita*, philosophy of the hedonist, every luscious fruit is picked and enjoyed right here and now, without any preliminary consideration of value nor estimation of consequences.

What, then, are the most important things? Let us start with the most obvious, the subjective center of the world and of all conscious thought : MYSELF. What am I? Who am I? Where am I going—if anywhere at all—and why?

A first psychological approach to the question was considered above. Let us start again from there and see how far we can go.

I am the son or daughter of parents, imperfect human beings who staggered through life in their own personal way, made their own mistakes, met their own failures and successes, were happy or unhappy through the interplay of heredity, fate, luck and a considerable number of free decisions, right or wrong, that made them be what and who they are. I was born of them without having been asked whether I wanted it or not. I had no choice as to my social, racial or national background, or as to the historical period in which I happened to appear on the face of the earth. In fact, I am here right now for a limited number of years, in this world of the twentieth century, in a given state of mental and physical development and health, and with a given number of social advantages and drawbacks.

Wisdom will consist in knowing myself and my inevitable surroundings as they are : they are good, relatively at least, for they are part of me, and anyway, they are all I have. A peaceful accounting is needed here, a count of my actual blessings instead of a revolt against fate's injustice, and the taking of revenge on myself through masochistic self-destruction, or on others through aggressive, sadistic, anti-social behavior. Nor should I condemn those who do take this negative road : some destinies are so tragic that they deserve infinite forgiveness and compassion.

Taking stock of ourselves, we are certain to discover we are not self-sufficient gods. In early infancy, we were utterly dependent upon our parents. Until our death, we will have to rely on the skills of butcher, baker and candle-stick maker if we are to lead a life that rises above the level of the stone age. The more civilized and intricate our culture, the more we will have to rely on the crafts and learning of others. A farmer may have learned all he needed from his father : he may continue to live on his land as in a closed and self-supporting society. By contrast, the city-dweller or the intellectual—scientist, artist, writer, teacher, priest—will have to be backed by countless other specialists who will satisfy his natural and intellectual needs.

But there are other needs of an even more essential nature : we crave affection, closeness, union, love. Love is basically outgoing, a call for the gift of- and to the other, a hunger for the fulfillment of our deepest desires through some form of communion, by immersion in an ocean of bliss. And so, we go out and communicate with others, and share our search and dreams with them. *If we are lucky and well-versed in the fascinating game of life, we will find true friendship and true love and go a long way toward happiness. But there will always remain a longing for more, for the beyond, for the absolute, for the perfect : and that is man's most important truth, and as we shall see later, it is hunger for God.*

Wisdom, then, will consist in appreciating ourselves objectively and joining others in the search for total happiness.

We live in a constant state of flux, a dynamic, rhythmic effort with its successive phases of progress and decay. Our own individual lives follow the pattern of all living things, great or small, from the most prestigious civilization to the tiniest insect : without having chosen to do so, we come into being, we live, we grow, we die. But at our level of being, there is a tremendous advantage : if we want to, we are in a great measure free to determine our own goal and our way to it.

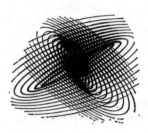

IMPROVING THE WORLD

THERE IS no use moaning over the world's imperfection, or that of men, including our own. Evil will persist until the end. Yet, we do not have to sit on the sidelines and watch the wretched world go by : we can act upon it, change it, improve it within the sphere of our own possible action, be it only within ourselves.

Concerning action on the outside world, an early word of warning is in order. Many well-intentioned attempts at "improving" the world around us have resulted disastrously in the exact opposite. We live in the age of the worst water- and air pollution in history. Countless times, short-sighted efforts toward improvement have resulted in long-range catastrophes. In spite of their science, scientists are responsible for ecological blunders from which some areas may never recover. To list but a few, insecticides are destroying wildlife at an alarming rate; the black flies of Canada, apparently imported to eliminate some other insect, have turned into a recurrent June plague; rabbits imported in Australia almost went out of control; and it was discovered lately by Captain Jacques Cousteau and his team that the good-intentioned introduction of trout in Lake Titicaca in South America resulted in the wholesale death of indigenous fish through some contagious fungus disease—with the potential upsetting of the whole way of life of the local tribes of Indians.

Trying to improve things is bad enough. Trying to improve people, at times against their will, in the style of the Inquisition, is often a false move based on ignorance and pride. Even the missionary spirit, so often based on genuine and dedicated love, has blundered at times by promoting the bad in both taste and doctrine while destroying much that was relatively good in local practices and beliefs. So let us not go out to improve the world of things and the world of men before we know what are doing, but let us take our little light from under the bushel and allow it to shine exactly as far as it can go. Who knows how many will see it and be comforted? That should be of no concern to us : " Ours only to do and die. " But this doing and dying may be much better than the violent deed and death of the men of war or the passive performance of the slaves : our doing and dying may be transformed into the love-deeds of men and women whom the truth has made free to do their thing as it should be done. Free from despair : for in the light of sacrificial love, the miseries of the world begin to make sense as occasions both of self-offering when we can alleviate them and of merit when we accept their inescapable burden. Free from death : " Death, where is thy victory, " when the final fire of life goes out in an outburst of love; when life on earth must end because the privation of total love has become unendurable? Free from anxiety and self-doubt : after all the care of our heart has been placed in the hands of Love, what more is there to worry about?

Yet, we still live in an imperfect, suffering, hurting world. No amount of love will ever do away with the pains of rebuke, frustration, ingratitude, misunderstanding, malice or plain stupidity. But the difference is that, with love in our hearts, these miseries will no longer be overwhelming : we will have learned to swim in the moving, salty, treacherous but exalting sea of mankind, to love it in spite of everything. If we ever do come to perfect wisdom, we will love it because of everything, for we will be able to see the striving behind the sin, frustrated hope behind despair, failures of love behind acts of malice, and infinite mercy covering them all.

This particular wisdom is the greatest of arts, for it is truth in action, truth brought to the level of the real, truth alive. Many are called wise, many more perhaps believe themselves to be so, who are but victims of their own confusion. For wisdom is often sought very foolishly, and there is no greater fool than a wise fool. It is the true wisdom of love that prompted the little holy ones—Francis of Assisi, Juan Diego, Joan of Arc, Bernadette Soubirous, Thérèse of Lisieux and many others—to be wise in the perfect fulfillment of their destinies, and in the humility of not trying to understand what was beyond their reach. As long as we are on earth, there is no full understanding, no definite answer, no final and complete wisdom, but only a constant choice between death and further striving. Any halting of the upward effort is in a sense a form of decay, for it is the loss of a potential act of love.

How much, then, should we strive and how high should we aim? This is a matter of balance and realism. We need both work and play. We need periods of utter relaxation, and, for those able to perceive them, flashes of edenic delight. No effort can be fruitful if pursued beyond the physical and nervous limits of the human organism. There is real wisdom in accepting this fact and conforming our lives to it.

As for the height of our aim, in one sense, it has no limit, and in another, it does have one. Our effort upward has no limit in the sense that man is made for ALL, for the full possession of the totally satisfying gift of his flowering humanity. How this can be achieved and what it ultimately means will be seen later. Our effort upward has a limit in its means : while striving for the infinite goal, we can proceed only by cautious and minute steps. Perfection exists in the final end. In everyday life, there is only imperfection, a routine, a grind of chores and minor labors, seemingly as remote from our ultimate goal as the worm is from the star. But the existential link, the redeeming factor, the human glory consist in seeing beyond the drudgery, in making of every pain and annoyance a sacrificial pebble, an offering added to the structure of our slowly growing self. We will be valued not so much by our heroic deeds as by our constant and faithful YES to life as it is, to our own personal life in the actuality of the here and now, the only life we have—which is also the best for us now precisely because it is the only one.

Perhaps the most practical approach to this form of wisdom consists in opening the avenues of contemplation. The objects of contemplation are as many as there are creatures. Everything we see or hear or taste or touch, everything we perceive may become a launching pad for the better understanding of our own privileged condition. A poet or a saint may help in this self-revelation, in this discovery of new worlds the supply of which is limitless.

One of the valuable approaches to contemplation in the natural order is concentration. Take an object—absolutely any object will do, but the works of nature are a richer source of discovery than those of man. Take a leaf, a blade of grass, a single petal from a flower, the smallest fragment of a butterfly wing, and concentrate on it as if you had never seen it before—which you most probably haven't anyway. Take the simplest and humblest one, the blade of grass. Think of what it means and is. Think of the inner forces of its growth and development, its fantastic chemical composition, its part in photosynthesis, in the cycle of life—your life—its adaptation to natural surroundings, its perfect design, the difference between inner and outer surfaces, the patterns of veins and structural supports, perhaps the razor-sharp teeth on its outer edge. Look at it under a microscope, and the wonder increases with the appearance of its cellular structure. There is no end to the contemplation of a blade of grass! As Walt Whitman said, " A mouse is miracle enough to convert trillions of infidels!" And Charles Morgan : " Knowledge is static, a stone in the stream, but wonder is the stream itself."

Starting from the contemplation of the simplest things, it is possible to rise to the greater harmonies of nature and to develop one of the main reasons for staying alive : a sense of constant wonder.

If one wishes to eliminate uncertainty, tension, confusion and disorder from one's life, there is no point in getting mixed up either with Yahweh or with Jesus of Nazareth.
ANDREW GREELEY

What was firm and certain has nowhere remained the ultimate.
KARL JASPERS

The price that man pays for consciousness is insecurity.
ERICH FROMM

I will have to get used to living without fences on the brink of an abyss that resembles me.
JEAN GIONO

Will you be surprised
when moments that have
forgotten to be announced
hit you hard and fast?
JUANITA

When the dominant myths of a culture are being fragmented by contradictions that can no longer be hidden, and when no new myths or rearrangements of myths have fully taken their place, an increasing number of persons become terrifyingly aware of the unstructuredness and naked freedom of human consciousness.
MICHAEL NOVAK

CHAPTER 3
METAPHYSICAL TRUTH:
PRECARIOUSNESS

THE MEANING OF METAPHYSICS

IMPORTANT AS THE PROBLEMS of psychological and logica truth may be, they do not go down to the deepest level of rationa understanding. They deal with perception, reception, acknowledgment of *something*. They consider this something in its immediately accessible characteristics, but never in itself. They are concerned with perceptible attributes only. For any understanding of the inner core of reality, we must have recourse to metaphysics—a much maligned word and an even more maligned science.

Because of the excesses of decadent Scholasticism juggling with ever-more abstruse notions, metaphysics came to be associated with unreality, vain and pointless discussions among men who had completely lost contact with life. Yet, considered as it should be, as the study of inner reality, metaphysics is most important. So important, in fact, that the lack of any relevant metaphysics is one of the major weaknesses of contemporary thought.

What, then, is metaphysics? The origin of the word itself is prosaic. It has nothing to do with any supernatural revelation or suprarational elucubration. Very simply, when Aristotle was in the process of organizing his thought, he placed at a certain point his book " On Physics. " The following book he naturally called " The Book After Physics, " or " Metaphysics. " So this is no highbrow consideration claiming to be over and beyond physical science, but much more modestly, that which, in Aristotle's scheme of thought, happened to come after the study of physical phenomena. There is then no fundamental antagonism between true science and true metaphysics : they are simply different approaches to reality, different disciplines.

Metaphysics is, specifically, the philosophical study of being as such. It is the study of what is left when we mentally strip reality of everything that makes it accessible to the senses; when we consider it in the abstract, outside of any spatio-temporal framework of actual existence. We examine, not this man, nor his race or mind or age or anything else, nor even the fact that he is a man, but the bare datum that he " is, " that he shares existence with a number of other beings and is thus in a state opposed to non-being.

The classical metaphysics of Scholasticism, even as expressed in nineteenth and twentieth century textbooks, is on the right track in that it emphasizes the importance of being, but it makes the general mistake of considering being as static rather than dynamic. It develops the study of the attributes of being, the one, the true, and the good, and of the relationship between essence and existence, potency and act, matter and form—that is, of what a thing can be and what it actually is, as seen under different aspects. This creates a valid discipline of reasoning on the basis of two postulates : that being is unchanging and that concepts have an absolute value. In classical metaphysics, the rules of logic are applied as rigorously as if terms had been mathematical symbols. This is done in the hope of obtaining absolutely true statements. In fact, as we have seen, no deductive reasoning has any more reliability than that of its terms. Nobody really understands comprehensively nor can anyone define perfectly any of the notions of classical metaphysics—except in a vacuum of abstract thought.

The main difficulty is always the same : nothing is properly definable, no-thing, that is, no actually existing reality. Beings on every level are in a state of flux. Absolute truths imply a contradiction in terms because there is an unbridgeable gap between the rigidity of any definition and the dynamism of the mind and of the thing defined. *A dogmatic expression, then, is at best that formula which, at one point of time and in a given language, expresses some fundamental fact which remains beyond total comprehension.* That is why there is so much danger in dogmatism, in the Churches and elsewhere. Any clan or school or rite or confession that claims exclusive possession of the truth is necessarily wrong because truth is still being formed in man. Even the most cherished and secure positions of our own faith are at best expressed through dogmatic definitions that will eventually have to be revised and enlarged. Should that make us doubt our religion or reject our faith?

Not in the least. No Church nor any man could possibly have a total and definite vision of anything—not even of a single grain of sand. Why, then, should we claim to possess the truth exclusively, and attempt to shove our definition of it down the throats of other people who may have their own ideas, more refined perhaps and better formed, though in a different language? All we can do—and this is the only sane position—is to be honest witnesses in our own existential attempts toward a true perception of whatever is.

THE METAPHYSICS OF PRECARIOUSNESS

AS WE have seen earlier, no acquired truth is ever in its final and absolute state of completion. Many a principle that had been thought to be simple and absolute turns out to be complicated and relative, and this both in the physical and the moral orders. Traditional doctrines are not to be discarded thoughtlessly, but neither are they to be swallowed whole.

What then can we hold on to? What security do we have? How can there be any metaphysics of the state of flux? How can any degree of rational order be attained if we are no longer today what we were yesterday—and God only knows what we shall be tomorrow!

The metaphysics of the state of flux will consist essentially in emphasizing *the importance of now*, as it happens to be, while accepting a different yesterday and providing for a different tomorrow. There is reality, security and certainty only as regards this present instant. *Metaphysical reality—being as such—is neither past nor future, but actual, and actually changing.* Instead of a meta-physics of essences and certainties, we will have to depend upon a metaphysics of precariousness, by far the wiser since it avoids the pit-falls of smugness and pride. *We are here, in a state of actual being, not as the final product of the act of creation or as the crowning and definite summit of evolution, but as the temporary product of the act of creating. We are here, not to rule and boast and remain forever : we are here at the trembling tip of the tentative evolution of life and love, present on earth for a moment and gone the next, and yet the bearers and representatives of what is best, most perfect, most advanced, the closest to the original dream of all-perfection as it exists in nature or in God.*

A metaphysics of precariousness will tell us that nothing is settled once and for all, nothing is solid or fixed, not even matter which consists in indefinable whirls within an immense vacuum; neither our sorrows nor our joys, neither our defeats nor our victories. Yet all things move toward a single end that it is our lifetime job to discover. A metaphysics of precariousness sees visible things as they are in truth; fundamentally unsettled, contingent, variable and vulnerable—which happens to be a very good definition of man. But it also sees them as existing possibly in a state relieved of the burden of precariousmess.

Hence, there are here notes both positive and negative. On the positive side, precariousness is the opposite of doom. If happiness is unreliable and fragile, so is unhappiness; if perfection is elusive and impermanent, so is imperfection; if virtue is fickle and liable to excess, so can vice turn into virtue. In a precarious, non-deter-mined world, there is always present the possibility of light-hearted, creative, unexpected joy, the fruit of freedom properly used. In a dogmatic and absolute world, punishment follows upon sin and reward upon virtue with a boring and unavoidable automatism. In a precarious world, everything depends upon the creative whims of free spirits. The burdens and pains are still real, but they too are precarious, subject to increase perhaps, but also to sudden alleviation and disappearance. The fate of man is not sealed : it is essentially of his own making. *Every man has the choice between indulging in self-pity or going out to fly a kite.*

A metaphysics of precariousness contradicts seemingly well-estab-lished patterns of behavior. If everything is changing all the time, and everything is liable to come to an end tomorrow or even this very minute, why live in a distant future, concentrating on retirement in five, ten, fifteen years? You may be retired peremptorily within the next few seconds. Why not enjoy this moment of your life as if it were the very last? Perhaps it is! Why not start doing right now all those things you want to do before you die? Another way of looking at it was expressed recently by a humorist : " Today is the first day of the rest of our life!"

If life is precarious, it is also exciting and new. And so, at this time of the evolution of the world, the outermost of the concentric cycles of wisdom seems to be that of freedom and joy, combined with passionate attachment to what is—NOW!

It is the mark of a generally educated mind not to expect a greater exactitude from any inquiry than the nature of that particular inquiry admits. ARISTOTLE

What he (the scientist) does not know seems to increase in geometric proportion to what he knows. Steadily he approaches a point where what is unknown is not a mere blank space in a web of words but a window in the mind, a window whose name is not ignorance, but wonder. ALAN WATTS

Science is human; it is of human devising and manufacture. It has not prevented war; it has perfected it. It has not abolished cruelty or corruption; it has enabled these abominations to be praticed on a scale unknown before in human history. LOREN EISELEY

What we have to deplore, I would say, is not that scientists are specializing but rather that specialists are generalizing. VIKTOR E. FRANKL

All the important things of life lie somewhere outside the sphere of the mathematically calculable. LIN YUTANG

Inconsistency, irregularity, novelty, surprise, mystery—all of which are not subject to scientific law—are as characteristic of nature as regularity. RAYMOND J. NOGAR

We are thus led to abandon the traditional notion of a strict determinism in observable physical phenomena and to substitute the much more pliable notion of a simple link of probability between them. LOUIS DE BROGLIE

Something unknown is doing we don't know what. EDDINGTON

CHAPTER 4

SCIENTIFIC TRUTH : PROBABILITY

THE NATURE OF PHYSICAL SCIENCE

THERE IS MUCH TALK in our days about the information explosion, the electronic computers, the new means of instant communication that seem to make so many methods of learning obsolete. Almost every educational publication is filled with the impact of technology on education, breaking sharply with the past. No modern University could do without a Language Lab, or several rooms filled with extremely expensive electronic gadgets. All this is presented as being of paramount importance, but its value seems highly exaggerated.

Human actions belong in two entirely different fields : the materially accidental and the spiritually personal, considered not as opposites, but as extreme poles. The fact that we happen to live in a world of physical change and growth forces us to defend our right to live and love.

There is a world of the physical scientist, and even of the behavioral scientist insofar as statistics have mathematical value. This world may be analyzed and computerized, reduced to data and tables that claim scientific objectivity and accuracy. However, the end-result of scientific analysis—inductive reasoning—is but a schematic vision of the rules of probability pertaining to certain aspects of the analyzable phenomena of material reality, whereas reality itself defies scientific investigation. What is offered by science is not a personal supply of truth which can serve as a basis for existential judgments, but an accumulation of figures representing totally impersonal data. It is out of a superabondance of such figures that modern man and woman are expected to build their visions and make their dreams come true. No wonder some of their visions turn into Dali landscapes, and their dreams into nightmares.

Some of the necessities of life, it is true, do not rise above the level of mechanization, automation and interchangeability. When it comes to manufacturing tools that will extend the range, power or perception of our physical senses—and this covers every appliance from a pair of eyeglasses to a jetliner—computerized data obtained from the physical world apply directly to the solution of problems of design and manufacturing. A TV set, for instance, does not have to be a masterpiece of creative craftsmanship, except in its prototype. If its parts are identical with those of a million other sets, it does not matter in the least : the only important thing is the quality of the picture. On the accidental and material level, modern science finds full justification : it provides us with an incredible range of marvelously delicate or powerful instruments.

But there is nothing in science that can serve as a guide to the proper use of these instruments. Science approaches reality with a cold, disinterested eye. To science, the thing is the end, and man is considered as a thing. The object of investigation needs no other justification than the fact that it is there, and no further moral rule than that it can be used in this way of that. The notion of " should" is absent from science. For moral guidance, we must look elsewhere.

Can the rules for the proper use of our new discoveries be elaborated without a return to the ancient books? This, again, would be doing things the hard way, taking enormous gambles, neglecting readily available sources of information because of the idolatrous adoration of novelty as such. That is where the importance of the humanities may be seen.

Yes, we live in the late nineteen-hundreds; yes, we are in the electronic, mass-production, thermo-nuclear age. But the only way to survival is the reaching of a sufficient level of general culture, a sufficient awareness of the riches collected by older generations, to enable us to cull from them the principles that will lead us to a true appreciation of our own time as seen, not in isolation, but in the perspective of history.

Perhaps specialization is a necessity of our age. The mass of available information has increased to such a point and at such a rate that the time is well past when a man could seriously compose a book entitled, " *Of Everything That Can Be Known.* " * But the

* The Italian scientist, Picus de la Mirandola (1463-1494). A later humorist, probably Voltaire, extended the title to make it read, " *De*

tragedy of our time is that specialists are frequently called upon to make decisions in fields of general human affairs, major policies or world politics. This weakness is offset in part by the broad use of consultation and committee decision. The fact remains, however, that besides the scientist, the specialist and the technician, there is room for the humanist, the man of vision able to see both backward in the past and forward into the possible future.

We have too many mad scientists, military experts, financial wizards, advertizing geniuses, and too few wise men. It is more than time that a greater number among the brilliant young, instead of being lured by the glitter of specialized techniques, become aware of the urgency of this other kind of service to humanity : overall culture and the search for practical wisdom. What they need most of all is the capacity to develop a program of study combining the proper material and the right kind of experiential contact with people.

THE IMPACT OF SCIENTIFIC DISCOVERIES

WHAT KIND of culture and wisdom are the average young exposed to? The eighteen-year-old American has absorbed about eighteen thousand hours of television. This evidently makes him or her different from teen-agers of earlier days. But does it make them any better prepared for life? Or any wiser? An objective look at what is being offered through the medium of this marvel of science reveals an appalling mediocrity in concepts, excessive violence and sadism, lack of respect for life, a flippant view of woman and marriage, obnoxious commercials, noisy and confusing

omni re scibili et quibusdam aliis."—" Of Everything That Can Be Known And A Few Others Besides."

cartoons. The marvel of science is being misused because of commercialism, appeal to the masses, and the scarcity of that imponderable and unscientific element : creative genius.

What will be the result of exposure to television in its present form? The child will be almost totally deprived of the occasions of solitude, inner development, contemplation, self-discovery. His sight and hearing will be so blunted by the flickering and screeching machine that he will no longer be sensitive to the more refined sights and sounds. What is offered to him comes with such powerful urgency that he cannot possibly escape. Instead of discovering his place in life through progressive natural processes, he will be flung into an artificial world controled by those whose major interest is to sell marchandise that is frequently useless and sometimes damaging. The latest report on the non-nutritive value of breakfast cereals is a case in point : some of the most heavily advertized are the least nourishing and the most popular!

Television is but one exemple of technology gone awry because of lack of wisdom in its use. When people destroy each other in car accidents, when bombs are dropped on confused peasants in the name of freedom, when the latest development of technology serves to thwart rebellion against technology, * it is time to think again, to place human development before gadgetry, moral values above scientific data and love before material gain. What is needed is a means by which to establish some logical relationship between the mass of information now being collected and the true needs of man. Statistical quantitative analysis, refined and elaborate as it may be, will never produce a human act, a human emotion, a human value. *There is as much difference between contemporary science and real life as there is between the Kinsey Report and a night of love.*

What is needed, then, is not pure technology stripped of any reference to older ways, but a better utilization of the discoveries of science. There should be organized a brain-tank of humanists able to draw the guidelines of true wisdom by keeping up with the flow of scientific data. The first names that come to mind for such a task would be Loren Eiseley, Mircea Eliade, Alan Watts, Viktor Frankl, John C. H. Wu, and, in an entirely different field, Hans Küng, Bernard Häring, Daniel Berrigan and Ivan Ilitch.

---

* A new chemical was recently demonstrated on TV : Its purpose is to make a street so slithery that a looter carrying a stolen TV could not make it across!

Because of the frantic pace of the scientific world, certain avenues of action are almost completely closed. Any patient, sustained, qualitative effort by creative individuals who need peace and quiet and space and time is impossible without rarely available financial sponsorship. Abundant funds are generally offered to institutional teams of scientists rather than to individual artists or creators in any field. By contrast, outstanding results are obtained in the physical sciences through the teaming of many minds, but a serious study needs to be made as to the proper objects of research. Millions are wasted on trivia or on war while basic human needs are neglected.

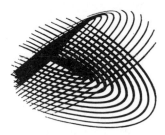

THE GOALS AND LIMITS OF SCIENCE

WHAT, and how much, should we know and seek to know? There is somewhere to be found a proper balance between the desire to know, the true and valid spirit of the new sciences, and respect for things beyond human reach. Some will claim that nothing exceeds the mind, that the mind is its own god. But let us be more humble and realistic and begin with an objective appraisal of our instruments of knowledge, and of the possible objects of knowledge.

The *range* of our intelligence is boundless because there is nothing toward which it is unable to extend. To know, in a sense, is to become the object known, to expand our being through the assimilation of other forms and other perfections, and thus to grow to a stature whose only limitations are those of the universe. We may know, share, even become in a way all that is, because there is no formal limit to the extension of our mind.

On the other hand, we are limited in the *quality* of our research by the four-dimensional boundaries of time and space. We are in natural contact only with things perceived through our sensory experience. This we then extrapolate through the process of abstraction in order to reach what we believe to be absolute ideas. But absolute ideas are in the rational order, and things in the existential order, and never the twain shall perfectly meet. Since our " absolute" ideas rest on nothing more than the rational analysis and comparison of phenomena perceived through more or less perfect senses and processed by a more or less imperfect intelligence, there is an intrinsic flaw even in the highest of our certainties because of an illegitimate passing from the order of appearance to that of reality. We believe we know a thing : all we know is how it felt, sounded, tasted, looked at a certain time and in a certain place. We never can know completely what it is.

Reality cannot be stopped at any given point and subdivided into analyzable fragments. As in the case of dissection, as soon as we consider any one part of the universe as separate and distinct from the whole, it ceases to function, to live, to be itself.

Furthermore, as we shall see later when considering the question of evolution, the universe is not a stabilized object offered to a static observer; it is a living, moving, changing, evolving, intersecting whole, in a sense surely creating itself, or at least continuing in the direction of the initial impulse. In medieval times, this had been expressed by St. Bonaventure among others as the progressive development of " seminal principles. " The conservative sees it as the work of providence, the Darwinian as an effect of the will to survive, and the Teilhardian, as complexification with an ever-increasing degree of consciousness (cerebralization).

Whatever the name or explanation, there is in the universe a form of growth both natural and mysterious that makes it proceed by leaps and bounds, progression and regression, through the interaction of countless forces in countless beings the resulting effect of which—the universe of now—is beyond comprehension. Love, cruelty, self-assertion, will, tension, gravity, all these combine into a single vital surge, a tremendous, stumbling and often blind effort towards something or someone. It is this same drive that makes all things and all men go, go, go.

In the midst of this extraordinary dynamic commotion, we the men of our age, coming after so many others, attempt to use the forces of intelligence. We are trying to make sense out of what appears to the defeatist as a meaningless and sickening mess. We apply our limited wisdom and growing science to solving the riddles of being, life and love.

Neat categories do not apply here : they serve merely to freeze minute particles of reality long enough to be observed. But since these categories themselves are created artificially out of inadequate abstractions, there is no possibility of reaching anything but glimpses of truth, tangential and fleeting contacts with things as they seem to be. In no scientific field can there be any absolute law.

The more we dig into reality, the more we come to realize how little we know about it. As a simple example, take the color white. To the primitive, white is white and that is that : there is no problem and no mystery. By looking a little closer, however, we come to realize that the color white results from the combination of all the colors of the spectrum. We are then faced with the problem of color : what makes green green or blue blue? The wave-length of light. But what is a wave, and what is light? Science discovers the photon, but what is a photon except a convenient word for the naming of a mystery? How does a photon act, as a wave or as a particle? Surprisingly, it acts both ways, and so both ways must be reconciled; and even if we can pull this trick, we are still just as far from knowing what light is.

The same difficulties are found in the attempt to understand anything else, and the problems become even more involved as we ascend the scale of being. Who can understand man? As for woman, every wise scientist has given up long ago!

And so, it is scientifically impossible to know anything totally, to possess it inside out, to be consciously aware of all that it was, is and could be. But is that any reason to be discouraged and to believe that rational analysis is of no value whatsoever? On the contrary, as soon as we have discovered its limitations, we are perfectly free to use it to the very brink of those limits we have been able to determine. *Even without absolute certainty, there is in scientific research such a high degree of probability that it may serve as a basis to solve the problems of every-day life.* But it is neither absolute nor sacred. Science is but one of the concentric cycles of wisdom, and not the final one. We have the task of developing it further, perhaps even, if we can, of discovering the next cycle that would encompass and reconcile earlier views and help resolve apparent contradictions. Science and religion are not mortal ennemies, but different approaches to one and the same reality.

It is impossible, then, to know any one thing perfectly, but it is quite possible to know something about anything, including the whole universe. For thousands of years, philosophers have been wondering how it all began. In the days of the Greeks and of their medieval interpreters, the problem was rather philosophical than physical, a matter or principles rather than of fact. The two main solutions proposed were : existence of the universe from all eternity, or creation in and together with time.

Aristotle proposed the idea that the universe was eternal. Thomas Aquinas never quite managed to dispel this notion : the closest he ever got to a denial was to teach that the eternal existence of the universe could not be disproved rationally. This infuriated some of his contemporaries, including Bonaventure of Bagnorea, who strongly asserted that matter must have been created in time.

There are two modern theories corresponding to these ancient views, populary known as the " Steady State" and the " Big Bang. " The proponents of the Steady State believe that matter always existed, and is in fact constantly being created at the same time as it is being wasted. They explain the apparent outward flight of the galaxies as one phase only of a gigantic pulsation by which the universe expands, only to return again upon itself, and expand again in an eternally recurring cycle. By contrast, the advocates of the Big Bang theory consider matter as having originated from a single point in space at a single instant in time, actually creating both space and time through the act of coming into being. Such are the only true modern cosmogonies.

Several marginal theories take for garanted the pre-existence of clouds of matter, nebulae, chaotic and disorganized elements. They are mere cosmologies, since they offer no solution to the question of how chaotic matter originated.

The material universe as we perceive it is constitued by an objective reality—something—which exists within the framework of a limited spatio-temporal relationship. Each of its components may be measured in terms of relative distance in relation to other things, and has the capacity of existing in different states of matter. Everything in the universe is capable of motion, which is spatio-temporal change, relative to its own inner parts and to other things.

But what is objective reality actually made of? Time and space are not realities in themselves; they cannot be experienced as such, but only in the form of relationships between things. They are not illusions, yet they do not exist as such, but only as existential limitations of something else in which they may be perceived.

If we imagine a given point at a particular instant of time and precisely determined within a system of three-dimensional coordinates, we do not have something existing in reality, but merely a concept, a potential locus for something else. What is it that " fills " this situation? One of the deepest mysteries of nature is perhaps the question of the solidity of matter. If we analyze its components, all that seems to remain is a maze of fields, forces, orbits, attractions and repulsions that do not seem sufficient to produce the solid substance of solid objects, since they appear as merely haphazard effects of nobody-knows-what wandering within proportionately immense spaces of emptiness. As against the naive nineteenth-century materialistic determinism which hoped to explain everything in terms of colliding billiard balls, the philosophy of modern physics must take into account the elusive reactions of mysterious particles whose solidity vanishes with every new discovery.

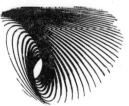

SCIENCE AND FAITH

NO BETTER conclusion to this chapter could be given than a summary of a short but profound paper by Dr William G. Pollard. * It came to my attention only after the chapter had been written, and is strikingly similar to the conclusions reached in the present work.

" What intellectual and cultural processes have resulted in the

* *Nature and Supernature* (unpublished, 1965). Doctor Pollard is at present Executive Director of the Oak Ridge Associated Universities, Inc., Oak Ridge, Tennessee. Quoted here with the kind permission of the author.

loss by modern man of an elemental capacity previously possessed
by the whole human race for response to that portion of external
reality transcendent to the order of nature?

" Until the rise of science in the seventeenth century, it was
not possible to make any clear distinction between natural and
supernatural orders. The whole aim of science is to seek natural
explanations of phenomena and structures. As long as science was a
minor activity in the whole society, carried out by a small minority,
it did not greatly affect the viewpoint or thought patterns of
the bulk of society. What is significant about the world today,
however, is the extent to which scientific styles of thought have
come to dominate the whole of society. The effect is to imprison the
spirit of modern man in three-dimensional space and time and matter
so that all reality which transcends the natural order effectively
vanishes from his apprehension.

" One of the most prominent changes we shall see is the slow
recovery of our lost capacity of response to supernatural reality.
I see a number of signs of such a trend, especially within science
itself. In every direction, science seems unbounded and open. Each
new mystery which it clears up becomes a starting point for a dozen
more. Science itself is reintroducing, at a much deeper and profound
level, the mystery, wonder and awe which were the universal
characteristic of man in all prescientific epochs. More and more
science itself is leading us to a sense of the contingency of nature
upon a range of reality transcendent to nature.

" The laws of nature as they are known and formulated are almost
entirely statistical in character. There are commonly several alternative modes of response in the same situation, and the laws
of science govern the probabilities for each of them. Because of
this statistical character of scientific law, the best that can be
done through science is to predict the most probable course of
events. But the really great and decisive moments in which the
major achievements of life and history are made are just those
which were least expected and most surprising in their occurrence.

" The supernatural dimension remains invisible and empirically
inaccessible. But if it were not there as an integral determinant
of the total event, there would be no harmony. Underneath all the
errors and superstitions which have grown up around this category
of experience, there is something real which only an age which
dogmatically rejects all supernatural reality could fail to grasp. "

Man's greatest happiness consists in exploring what is explorable and revering what is not.

WOLFGANG VON GOETHE

Whatever people may pretend, everyone knows that he is in the dark in regard to the things that matter. Those that have any light only know enough to understand their ignorance better than others—and know that their ignorance is not a knowledge but a faith. You will say that this is mysticism, but I suppose that the mystics are those who are nearest to knowledge about the hidden world. We must remain content to see darkly.

ERIC GILL

...to know that what is impenetrable to us really exists, manifesting itself as the highest wisdom and the most radiant beauty.

ALBERT EINSTEIN

Be careful now to believe and trust, and in the end you will see it all in its fullness and joy.

BLESSED JULIAN OF NORWICH

The heart has its reasons which reason knows not. This is felt in a thousand ways. It is the heart that perceives God, not the mind. Such is perfect faith : God perceived by the heart.

BLAISE PASCAL

The believer will open his mind to the faith on condition that it fits in with his preconceived ideas and wishes. Faith, on the other hand, is an unreserved opening of the mind to the truth, whatever it may turn out to be.

ALAN WATTS

CHAPTER 5

RELIGIOUS TRUTH: MYSTERY

THE THREE LEVELS OF FAITH

EITHER WE LIVE by faith or we die—of fear, frustration, anguish, tension. There are three necessary levels of faith: the *practical* in the order of the instruments we use, the *personal* in the order of our relations with people, and the *supernatural* in the order of first origin and last end.

At almost every step of contemporary life, we are required to make acts of *practical faith*, generally explicit but at times quite conscious. Who has ever ridden an elevator in a high-rise building without making an act of faith in the tensile strength of the cable? It is impossible to drive a car without faith in it—which is indirectly personal faith, in the engineers who designed it, the technicians who built it, the service-men who keep it going. Our safety on the road is entirely dependent upon them: a loose nut, an imperfect linkage, a faulty fluid line may very well mean our sudden death. If we begin to think of all the possible mistakes in car design, construction and maintenance, we will never have the courage to drive. The same is true of many of the daily instruments we use.

Faith in this order is a tremendous short-cut, a saver of effort and anguish, but it is valid only as long as its object is worthy of it. We are in fact perfectly right to give general confidence to our car, while keeping our eyes open to possible defects. This is the kind of faith we need for everyday living: a well-founded, cautious and qualified trust in things, without which modern life would be impossible. We are forced to use many gadgets and implements the inner workings of which we would be quite unable to check, let alone understand—for instance, our TV set. There is a great difference between a timid and fearful man without faith and a critical skeptic. The timid and fearful will accept nothing at all;

the critical skeptic will accept nothing on its face value. A sound measure of skepticism is a condition of wisdom and even survival, for it is the reasonable reaction to the advertizing claims of an imperfect world.

At a higher level of our existence, we are bound to make many acts of *personal faith*—faith in people, husband or wife, children, relatives, co-workers or the man in the street. The matter is complicated by the natural impenetrability of the person : no one can get into another's head. His thoughts are his own, and so are his motives—and his actions are free and unpredictable at least in part. How, then, will it be possible to survive in a world of men and women? Our faith in people is based on our personal knowledge of them and on the statistically probable behavior of those we do not know. Through remembered reactions in similar circumstances, we can predict with sufficient practical accuracy what people are going to do. The closer we are to them, the more we love them, the more accurate will be our faith in them. There are some seeringly conscious instances of such personal faith : for instance, our faith in a surgeon into whose hands we deliver our very lives.

There is yet another and still higher level of faith, *supernatural faith*—belief in our total being and destiny. It is concerned with who we are, where we are going, and why. This is what Paul Tillich calls " the dimension of depth. " * All the important questions of life are a matter of depth and mystery. The very first concerns our own selves. We never really know who we are, we must take ourselves on trust, we need faith in ourselves, confidence in our powers, otherwise inertia and despair await us. We must also believe that our life makes sense as a whole, that the world exists for a purpose of which we are part—as much as possible a consciously contributing part—and that it is not doomed to absurdity. Many things in the world do seem absurd, but is the whole thing a joke? Either the universe and everyone of us within it are worthless and meaningless riddles and everything and anything goes until we die of horror—or it is, and we are, a wonderful, dreadful, breath-taking mystery that has an answer, a raison d'être, a solution beyond absurdity.

Is it wise to live in a state of natural optimism, to believe in this

* " The Lost Dimension in Religion, " in " Adventures of the Mind, " Vintage Book, New York, 1960, p. 52.

drang nach leben, this drive toward immortal life? Has anyone throughout history lived in this way and found happiness? The writings of the saints and mystics are one long ecstasy, pain and joy, suffering and delight combining in the most extraordinary paradox. There is no doubt either about the no less real if less spectacular happiness of men and women of peaceful virtue who live by faith, hope and love. If we look into ourselves, we perceive different urges, attractions and repulsions, emotions and feelings that result in the production of that amazing " I " which had started out as a pair of cells, changed into a kicking and gurgling lump of sensual needs, and evolved into a thinking and participating man or woman. This in itself is an amazing victory over pessimistic doubt. Man, indeed, is risen from the deep. As Teilhard de Chardin sees him, he is the finest flower of the tree of life with a tremendous potential for future growth.

Whatever man's material circumstances, there is always some avenue open to progress. In the concentration camp or in the ghetto, in the grind of industrial slavery or the grip of physical disability, even under the material and moral torture of war, there remains some possibility of assertion of the indomitable human spirit. Only when that spirit is broken does faith die away, but a broken spirit is no longer responsible morally. If the breaking has come about through human cruelty or any other circumstance beyond the subject's control, he will have passed beyond the area of God's justice into that of his mercy. This is no imaginary solution, no application of some unfounded other-wordly belief, but part of faith and a consequence of the sense of order in this world.

If we look at our neighbor, we come to realize that faith, or mutual trust, is a sure sign of the civilized life. As soon as we are no longer forced to keep vigil against man and beast in order to stay alive, as soon as we can put down the club, the stone ax, the bow, the gun—not to mention the hydrogen bomb—there is realised an immense energy that can be used for better things. Think of the waste in lives and materials brought about by recent and contemporary wars. Think of the progress that would have been possible in the order of human welfare if the potential wasted in the development of sophisticated weaponry had been channeled into it. On this count, the level of our civilization is pitifully low if we consider the insecurity of our city streets and the state of international relations. We have too little faith in our brother, and he has too little faith in us, and there is in both instances a lack of love because of the lack of understanding.

There will always remain a dross of sin, cruelty, envy, malice and lust. It should not be confused with life itself, as if life were essentially corrupt, as if there were in man no underlays of courage, goodness, kindness and desire for peace. It may be both dangerous and self-defeating always to act defensively, as if there were always some evil intent in the back of the other's mind. Such an attitude is unfortunately characteristic of international diplomacy : never do the representatives of any one country seem to be given the benefit of the doubt by the representatives of any other—particularly if there is between them some man-made iron, silk, bamboo or other curtain or some difference in race, culture or creed. Since some such differences exist between any two men and any two countries, it leads to universal distrust. A political group, a race, a nation are marked as " the enemy" on the flimsiest ground, and immediately accused of every sin. This is necessary to foster righteous fervor for " our" side and justify violence and cruelty against the other. The falsity of the status of" enemy" may be seen in the instant turnabouts of international politics : as soon as a war is over, our ex-enemies become our best friends as in the case of Japan and Germany. Conversely, nothing worse can seemingly happen to a country than to be" helped" as our allies, as is evident enough in Vietnam.

Some of the power and efficiency of Good Pope John, and perhaps also of the late President Kennedy, derived from their having been sensitive enough to human good will to make people act with more honesty and intensity than they had intended originally. There is a quality of faith that brings about a response of faith upon which it is possible to build marvels. Distrust a man, and he will muff the task you assigned him; give him credit for what you hope he can do, and he will quite possibly do it well. And love your enemies : they could very well become your closest friends. By contrast, treat a man as an inferior, and he will set your world on fire—next time, or this time.

FAITH IN GOD

AND NOW about God. Is there such a thing as life-giving faith in God, or is this a meaningless expression? Faith in God is a gift. It is offered to those who seek him in all good will and objectivity, knocking at the door of truth, hoping for an answer. The knocking may take a lifetime, or the door may open at the first approach. There is no human reason why faith is so hard for some men and so easy for others : the ways of God are not the ways of man. " It is vain for you to rise early, or put off your rest, you that eat hard-earned bread, for he gives to his beloved in sleep" (Psalm 126). But the gift of faith, if earnestly sought, is always offered somewhere, somehow, for God will not be vanquished in generosity and love.

What, then, is the gift of faith? It is not merely intellectual assent to a set of dogmas, but much more than that : the YES attitude, a whole program of life, a renewal, an inner transformation that makes everything pass into a level of reality immensely more substantial and actual than the superficial contacts of ordinary days. It is generally the fruit of a deeper plunging into life, not of isolation in some hermitage. Too often what is found in solitude is nothing but the sterility of the isolated mind. Isolation is good only so long as it is a means of deeper involvement into the needs of men.

The fundamental element of the gift of faith in God is the ineradicable certainty that everything makes sense in the long run because the only reality is love. The nature of love will be considered later. Here it is seen merely as an object of faith. Faith, in this context, is a way of life that consists in accepting love, or at least the possibility of love, in everything and everyone. Even the " fat lady" is Christ, as Salinger expresses it so well. We may in fact be surrounded with pitiful, pretentious, foolish, ugly, blundering fat ladies and fat men, thin ladies and thin men—no gentle ladies nor gentlemen, but plain, ordinary people of every race and mental attitude, hawkish or peaceful, brilliant or uneducated, enlightened or darkly possessed by prejudice and hatred. Faith allows us to see God through them : to pierce the black cloud of hatred and discover a wounded ideal, penetrate the sullen masses and undestand that if they have so little to give it is mainly because they have received so little. Such a vision is truly Christ-like, and it is also the only remedy to despair at the sight of humanity as it is.

Faith in God allows us to see the spark of courage, goodness, patient love, brotherly kindness in the poor, the oppressed and the apparently wicked. It allows us also to see it in the rich and the powerful, although the effort may be greater and the harvest less abundant. They too are part of suffering humanity but their vaster privileges and greater opportunities of evil demand on our part a greater amount of understanding and love.

Faith in God reveals to us the powerful surge of life itself. It shows us that it is good, that the earth is good and everything in it. All this supposes that God exists. This, then, raises two questions : Does God exist? If he does, what are we to do about it?

Many a brave and imprudent man has wasted his time and energy trying to prove or disprove the existence of God. Their error is to have assumed naively that God could be made into an element of rational argumentation, a necessary conclusion to some inductive or deductive process. As we have seen, neither form of reasoning is able to produce absolute certainty. Furthermore, any being that could be encompassed by human thought could not at the same time be God. Reason cannot prove its own reason. *An existent cannot give proof that it exists : it is that proof.* There is then, by necessity, no valid logical or theological proof of the existence of God. But there is an overwhelming intuitive and mystical evidence in favor of it, backed historically by biblical revelation, and established existentially by the abundant fruits gathered by those who assumed he was the most important factor in their destiny.

Does this mean there never was any doubt in the minds of the saints? On the contrary, the holiest men and women were often assailed by the heaviest temptations of doubt. They were unsure not only as to whether God had anything to do with them, but even as to whehter he existed at all.

Some people seem to have made a kind of mental covenant : " Dear God, if you exist, prove yourself to me and I will believe." This is self-defeating arrogance. It eliminates the very point where merit comes into the search : the gratuitous offering of self, total abandonment to whatever or whoever God may be.

The highest level of faith coincides with the obstinate, unreasoned and immediately unrewarding adherence to the very last shred of belief

*in the real existence of the God of love, in spite of suffering, horror,
and the icy abandonment of the Dark Night of the Spirit, that final
and most dreadful test of the lover of God. For " blessed are those
who have not seen, and yet have believed".*

What can we know about God through faith? It is hard to
worship a vast and shadowy figure roaming through history, a
chance Omnipotent Power, an unattainable First Mover, an
incomprehensible Pure Act. God is the direct object of mountains of
volumes of theology. On reading them, one is reminded of a passage
in the Bible where Elijah meets God on Sinai : " And behold, the
Lord passeth. And a great and strong wind before the Lord, over-
throwing the mountains and breaking the rocks in pieces : the Lord
is not in the wind. And after the wind an earthquake : the Lord is not
in the earthquake. And after the earthquake a fire : the Lord is not
in the fire. And after the fire a whistling of gentle air..." (III Kgs.
20 : 11-21). The Lord is in the gentle breeze. " And the Word was
made flesh and dwelt among us" (John. 1 : 14). The gentle air had
become the gentle man, the Christ of the Beatitudes. And the most
amazing thing about it, as someone said recently, is not that Christ
could be God, but that God could be Christ.

The whole thing is magnificently, stupendously incredible. The
message of faith and love and simplicity is so much against the
grain of human passion that its proponent was quickly sent to the
gallows. Yet, millions of people are still living by the word of this
man who said, " I am the way and the truth and the life" (John. 14 :
16)

What of the historical criticism of the Gospels? What of all this
talk about " demythologizing"? Is the faith of ages of Christianism
to be reduced to the level of a consoling fairy tale? Historical
criticism is superficial and accidental when compared to the substantial body of evidence in favor of the reality of Christ. Using the
methods of some of the critics, it would be easy to prove Napoleon
never existed. The figure of Christ may have been blurred, some of
the sayings attributed to him are perhaps apocryphal, others may
have been misinterpreted, but there is overwhelming evidence to
prove his existence as a man of all-surpassing moral perfection.
But was he, is he, God? Every true Christian is willing to stake his
life on the belief that he is.

But what of the difficulties, the Immaculate Conception, the
Virgin Birth, the " brothers" of Christ? What possible connection

can be established between the son of a young Jewish girl and the Second Person of the Trinity—supposing there is a Trinity, and supposing there is a God? This again is a matter of faith. What if proponents of different theories disagree on essential points of doctrine? There is one perfectly satisfying and appeasing attitude that will take care of it all : the peaceful acceptance of God's truth, whatever it may be in fact, without regard to any of its imperfect dogmatic expressions. There is no need to understand the inner functioning of the Trinity : no one does. Nor is there even any need to understand the possibility of the Trinity : no one does either. All that is required of the religious man of good will is a personal assent to whatever is the beginning and end, the fundamental explanation and reason of what we are. Call it even MAN if you like : the name is unimportant so long as you are seeking the reality of life and love in its highest form. The word God itself is but a name for the Unnamable One. In Christ alone do we have a perceptible object of worship. If we may worship man, it is because in Christ humanity itself was made worthy of adoration.

Faith in God implies no indignity, no humiliation, no surrender of our inner freedom to some autocratic power, but simply the yielding to fact, the recognition that what is is, the perfectly civilized and gentlemanly bowing before the foundation and essence of what we are.

Once the general assent of faith has been given, we are faced with another question : what are we supposed to do about it? If the reality and presence of God in the world are accepted as facts, they should be acknowledged in some human way and integrated into the general framework of human existence. Now, this existence is both personal and social, so that we will have an obligation to do something personally and socially. Personally, we must investigate the documents of revelation—the Gospels principally— and conform our way of life to their inner logic. Socially, we must participate in community worship. For centuries, community worship has been practiced differently by different Church groups that shunned intercommunication. In the last few years only have they begun to come together to share each others' wealth.

Should we discard the imperfect shells of the Churches as we know them, and live by the inner core of our faith? Should we make up our own rites and worship in the personal cell of our individual spirit? This would be prideful and dangerous. It might have worked had we been alone, but we are not. In other fields of life, men do not go out on their own : they first look around to find out how things are being done traditionally. Only then do they try to improve some practice. The same should apply to our worship. Before starting a cult of our own, before deciding precisely what to do in response to the fact that we are not the supreme power and perfection of the universe, let us have a look at what others have done before us and are still doing now. Let us at least give a chance to Organized Religion by checking its origin and its fruits. *

Since we live in communal groups—families, business associations, cities, nations—there is much sense to be found in religious community functions on levels corresponding to them : family devotions, parochial, diocesan or Churchwide activities. Religion—our relations with the mystery, the numinous—does not consist essentially in these fragmented functions, for it is related to one single whole in which we live and breathe and have our being, but whatever we do in a practical way about religion has to be channelled into something which corresponds to our everyday life.

But is there a True Church, and how can we find it when all claim to be " IT " while contradicting each other on major points of doctrine? Such contradictions do not prove every Church to be wrong on everything; nor do they prove that if one Church is right, or righter, every other is necessarily wrong on everything. They merely serve to determine the areas in which there is a greater need for understanding and charity. The attitude of total intransigeance characterized the councils of Trent and Vatican I as it did their opponents, the Reformers. We are now in the age of Vatican II when the concern for pastoral love has overcome the stress on technically impossible definitions of the indefinable. We have come to understand that many apparent contradictions between opposing Churches are often misunderstandings rather than doctrinal errors, misinterpretations rather than valid arguments, historical blunders instead of differences in belief. We are now living in the exciting age of ecumenism : for the first time in history, the proponents of different forms of worship are looking at each other with open charity instead of closed hatred, and this is a giant step forward.

The choice of a Church is ours to make. Many are those who made

* This question is further developed pp. 139 ff.

this choice before us, and their response may serve as a guide. In a matter of such gravity, it is not enough to follow family traditions, a first personal impulse, or a superficial feeling of like or dislike. The choice must be mature, well-prepared and abundantly documented. We must read and study with conscientious thoroughness and attention. But in the end, the decision will have to be our own. There will always remain before us a chasm of doubt, some final abyss over which we will have to jump. Perhaps this final jump will be impossible, leaving us uncommitted until death, for faith is a gift. But what is more important than total assent and belief is the willingness to accept the truth, whatever it may be and in whatever way it is revealed to us, even if we cannot and do not understand it all. And no religious truth can ever be understood in full. NOW is the time to say in the depth of our conscience : " Lord, whoever you are, and in the measure in which you exist at all, I believe : help my unbelief!"

CONCLUSION: THE DIFFERENT LEVELS OF TRUTH

LET US now compare the different sources of possible truth in terms of their level of certainty.

Mathematical Truth was seen to be certain because of its strict confinement in the order of quantity alone, and the valid application of the laws of deductive reasoning.

Logical Truth (Symbolic Logic) could be relied upon only as long as the operations of syllogistic reasoning were limited to the use of abstract symbols. As soon as concepts and terms were inserted, some doubt set in because of the impossibility of passing from the order or mental and verbal analogical symbolism to that of concrete reality.

Metaphysical Truth reached its highest point with a statement concerning the wisdom of precariousness.

Scientific Truth was reduced to practically useful but only statistically probable rules of apparent measurable behavior of material beings.

Can there be any greater certainty in the final possible source of truth, intuition, the *Truth of Faith?*

Intuition itself, as the etymology indicates, is a kind of inner vision. Its inwardness is twofold : the vision is perceived within the intimate depth of the subject, and it seems to reveal the intimate depth of the object. Yet, it is far from infaillible since visions may be illusory. Intuition is in the same order as mystical insight, beyond logic and reason, and seems to be particularly a feminine gift. It consists in an existential contact with reality that bypasses the need for rational symbolic representation, providing a sudden light upon certain aspects of being. It may be seen as an act of emergence out of sterility and death into superluminous life. It cannot, however, be relied upon as a common source of truth, since in its highest and most perfect form that procures true knowledge it is an uncommon gift founded on extensive preparation and meditation. Sometimes, however, it seems to appear out of the blue. Most of the great works of science and art were the fruit of some intuitive urge beyond rational analysis. In religious terms, this may be seen as the action of the Holy Spirit responding to the openness of the human mind.

The intuition of faith is similar to that of creative art in that it, too, exceeds the limits of reason. Its object is specifically the assent to mystery. Faith, however, is not the solitary exercise of the individual mind : there is a body of beliefs, a corpus of faith, elaborated by mankind in the course of history, divided into the different branches of the major " faiths. " But different faiths have different and often contradictory teachings. How, then, can we distinguish the truth? Which teachers can we trust?

We may have confidence in the happy ones, the bright ones, the luminaries of human civilization and progress, the kind and humble, the generous and good, the wise and saintly—those who practice the perfection of what they preach and prove its rightness through their lives. Even to them, we should give no more than critical faith, checked and controlled and limited to that much assent which seems reasonable. Under these precautionary conditions, a careful study of the written documents of human wisdom will procure a sound basis for our life.

But even after reading all the works of the wisest of the wise and the saintliest of the saints, we will have no blinding certainty, for the deeper we delve into the reality of man, the more profound is the mystery of ourselves, and the more apparent the need at one point of an all-out gamble : the choice between YES and NO. Yes or no to life, to love, to personal sacrifice, to the notion of man rising gloriously toward some unimaginably lofty goal. And everything within us cries out toward life and splendor.

PART III

THE THEOLOGICAL PROBLEM
OF PERSONAL LIFE

What is Love?

When at the empty dawn of all creation, God created the primal essence, energy, he endowed it with such subtle, miraculous potencies that, as from a seed that slowly comes to flower, there grew from it what we call space and time and matter and radiation. What little we understand of the world is yet enough to reveal a sublime harmony beneath its turmoil and complexity. BANESH HOFFMANN

Every scrap of our knowledge derives its meaning from the fact that we are factors in the universe and are dependent upon the universe for every detail of our experience.
ALFRED NORTH WHITEHEAD

There is in me no simple form, but a form necessitated by the cohabitation of all the other forms of the universe.
JEAN GIONO

The act of creation is a divine lark by which the Persons of the Trinity chose to embody, in a discrete and granular world, an analogical reflection of their own mutuality.
ROBERT FARRAR CAPON

You say, " I came into this world. " You didn't : you came out of it, as a branch from a tree. ALAN WATTS

We start out with hope, faith and fortitude—they are the unconscious " no-thought " qualities of the sperm and the egg, of their union, of the growth of the foetus, its birth.
ERICH FROMM

If evolution be extended to everything, there must be something implicit in undeveloped matter or organisms, which will later be revealed. MARTIN CYRIL D'ARCY

We do not know what God has to say to man. We are all children of the universe and I would deeply love to believe there's some purpose which will be revealed to us.
HERMAN KAHN

CHAPTER 1
EVOLUTION : HUMANITY AND THE INDIVIDUAL

THE ORIGIN OF MAN

THE FINAL PROBLEM of man consists in finding the rules of righteousness, discovering what is good for him in the short run and in the long. The rules applying to any being depend upon its origin. What, then, is the origin of man? Undoubtedly, man is a product of natural evolution.

Evolution, as a theory of biological progress, is being confirmed almost daily by the discoveries of paleontology. The biological origin of man is being pushed into a past so distant that it staggers the imagination. The biblical story of creation in " six days" at a time about seven thousand years before Christ is purely symbolical. The events of the creation of the universe and of man are billions of years apart, and the appearance of erect, rational man on earth seems to have occurred at least a million years ago.

The materialistic geneticist sees evolution as the mathematical result of the interplay of chemical laws and probability. For the spiritualist, the living being is not the result of laws and chance alone. It is not chemistry and probability alone that have resulted in the progressive combination of more and more complex mollecules, evolving into living cells, and, after millions of years of slow transformation, into the intelligent vertebrates we have become. For the spiritualist, all this was preplanned, made part of the nature of matter, built so to speak into the physical elements, so that the rise of intelligent life had been intelligently foreseen. Evolution is not a blind struggle for the survival of the fittest, but the development—automatic in its processes—of a rationally conceived plan.

The original act the notion of which recurs constantly in human

thought, the " beginning, " the " first day, " or, in terms of traditional religious thought, " creation, " may be seen in this light, not
as a succession of acts of prodding, pushing and bringing forth by
some busy-body God, but as the breathtakingly single and simple
act out of which everything received the possibility of being :
out of which everything could be made to rise from the initial
thrust. We do not have to imagine a creator interfering in every
motion or change or presiding over every birth : and yet, every
motion and change and birth is part of that single act of willing-
doing which was at the origin of all things. It is because that act
is one that everything may be traced to a single source, and for the
same reason that all things are interrelated. They came forth from
one point, they follow one pattern, they will come to one end,
to one accomplishment and fulfillment.

Let us consider this viewpoint at least as a possibility, as opposed
to the view of materialistic science that sees matter as being its
own cause, depending upon itself alone, and going blindly along the
ways of chance to some dark and unimaginable doom—or to the
despair of a constantly recurring cycle.

The Darwinian theory of the origin of species has been demonstrated in a number of animal groups that show through skeletal
variations the progressive stages of development from one level
into another. The Museum of Natural History in New York, for
instance, shows a series of skeletons, from the so-called eohippus that
must have looked like a large hare or a small antelope, to the modern
horse. The series could have extended further by demonstrating
evolution from earlier species, going perhaps through the great
reptiles, the fishes, primitives worms and even lowlier forms of
life. The inescapable conclusion follows : the modern horse is not
a finished product. It seems to be a fixed species only because of
the relatively short span of scientific observation. No scientist
ever was a witness to an evolutionary change, so that traditional
science came to believe in the stability of the species, founded on
a philosophy of the stability of essences.

In the case of man, some lines of evolution have been clearly
drawn, although with less continuous evidence than in the case of
other animal groups. There are gaps, missing links, incertitudes
concerning the order of derivation. Yet, the general principle is well
established : man evolves along the same general pattern as all other
living beings and shares with them his remotest origin. The critical

question, however, is how and since when man attained his present state of rational intelligence, freedom and responsibility.

If man had always existed in his present form, all we would have to do would be to establish the rules of a corresponding morality, express it in absolute form, and perpetuate the knowledge of it for future generations. But if man is still evolving, the question of ethics is no longer one of static absolutism, but of dynamic adaptation.

Can any precise point be discovered where man became suddenly this completely different being, this rational dreamer of immortality, this creative bearer of love? Such things are so superior to mere animality that it was easy to suppose that they had occurred as the result of one single evolutionary leap—the sudden passing into a different and higher state. This corresponds with the traditional theologian's theory of the creation of the soul. In fact, did pre-man become man as the result of a single act of nature or of God, or did this happen by imperceptible degrees without any determinable threshhold?

Man does not seem to have been from the very beginning the perfect realization of some abstract essence. The vision of Adam unfolding in the full glory of his manly youth, able to reason and speak with God, naming animals to show his dominion over them, has no historical counterpart in the groveling, cave-dwelling, hirsute and prognathic creatures whose remains are being dug up in the Olduvai Gorge and elsewhere. Yet, there seems to be no doubt that these beings were men. Out of this primitive form—which in all probability came after many other forms, all the way down to the origin of life—man has become the xxth century manipulator of H-Bombs and LSD. His true essence—if such a term may be used in an existential progressive context—is to be found, not in some immutable " idea " pre-existing in nature or in God, but in that which he happens to be right here and now.

Ethics, then, the art and science of rightful human behavior, must be based, not on some a priori picture of what man is supposed to be, but on the a posteriori fact of what he actually is.

GENERAL AND INDIVIDUAL EVOLUTION

THERE IS a striking parallel between the general evolution of the human race and that of each individual man, in that every one passes through all of the evolutionary stages before becoming truly and fully himself. He starts out as did most life by being a combination of two living cells, develops through multiplication of these cells and emerges at birth as a physiologically complete infant. At each of these stages, he corresponds to some species of life as it exists in nature in an arrested form : the amoeba, the radiolaria, the worm, the fish, the mammal. All this is well known. But what seems seldom to have attracted the attention of the observer is that the parallel does not cease with birth : the child continues to grow along the same lines as historical mankind.

The first instincts and mechanisms to develop are those indispensable for survival, respiration and nutrition, blood and lymph circulation, assuring also the growth and development of the individual. The senses become active, establishing contact with physical phenomena in the outside world. These in turn are acted upon by the rudiments of association and thought. The child passes progressively in an evolutionary manner from the state of physiological animality to that of human rationality. A very young child closely resembles primitive man : instinctual, self-centered, violently passionate, concerned mostly with its own well-being. Thought develops as a luxury, over and above these basic needs. In its early stages, thought is still closely related to the senses : its gamut covers hunger and thirst, comfort and discomfort, warmth and cold considered not as abstrations but as present facts. The child at this stage is a primitive existentialist concerned exclusively with the here and now and their directly perceptible effects, good or bad.

Then affection begins to play its part. The sources of welfare are identified, and there is an emotional going out to them, consisting in both gratitude for favors received and propitiation in the hope for more. This is the beginning of sociability and love. The child gives itself to its parents, feeling in union with them, partaking in the security of assured support. This original security is of prime importance for the harmonious psychological development of the future man.

Continuing the parallel, the child passes from an instinctual-affective stage to one of symbolical abstractions. Less palpable notions are recognized. Different and more subtle goods receive a name, an identity—and also different and more subtle evils. They come to be emotionally associated with situations or persons. In the development of humanity, there is a similar stage : that of symbolical anthropomorphism in which all forces, good and evil, are first named, then given a human face.

Later, abstract thought develops, principles begin to be perceived and the power of reasoning is acquired progressively. At this point, reality assumes a well-defined neatness, things falling into black or white categories of good or evil, right or wrong, agreable or disagreable. There are few nuances or qualifications. Judgments are passed with candid absoluteness : there is no more rigid dogmatic theologian than an early teen-ager. The corresponding stage in the development of mankind is " the age of reason," the metaphysical stage, supported by the uncritical certainties of billiard-ball physics.

Later still, the shaded areas of doubt appear between the full light of truth and the total darkness of error. Judgments become qualified, intelligence and will learn to be humble and somewhat hesitant. This is a sure sign of maturity—and it comes from contact with mystery, the " other," the unconceivable, the unfathomable ocean of the unknown.

At this point the ways diverge, as they do in modern philosophy, leading either to confusion or to wisdom. The non-initiated, having lost the metaphysical props of dogmatic absolutism, can see nothing but chaos in the apparent irrationality of the world as it is. He lacks perspective, a cosmic vision, faith in an order that exceeds the range of sensory perception and even that of human intelligence. When things do not turn out as he hoped they would, he believes the sky is falling.

By contrast, the initiated has a much broader outlook. His line of sight is not blocked by local failures, temporary defeats, daily injustice or suffering. He is still affected by them but no longer overwhelmed, for he is able to see beyond the immediate disorder a majestic and universal hope in the future of growing and groaning humanity. He considers past and present anguish as mere birth-pangs introducing the promise of a better life. His longing extends both to order and beauty in this world and to an eternity of happiness in the next—and he devotes his life to the hastening of their advent. This is as far as humanity has been able to reach, this is the present status of its lovely people, the active prophets of faith, hope and love. The child has now become a fully mature adult : humanity has at least a clear vision of better things to come.

For the initiated, there is in the world of nature a pattern of growth and long-term harmony, a logical expansion and organization that no amount of random evolution could ever explain. The very laws of evolution need a reason : their existence implies an antecedent plan. In nature, we see some astounding results of this plan, but we never come face to face with the planner.

The world as we consider it at both extremes, the microscopically small on the sub-atomic level and the macroscopically enormous on that of the galaxies, suggests a further reality. It proclaims in its own way that it is neither self-made nor self-intended, that it must be good for something else. It flashes frequent signals, intelligent and intelligible. As soon as the mind receives them, it tries to trace them to their source. * Whence the immensity, the order, the splendor? Those who have reached the highest development of mankind discover here a sign of their God.

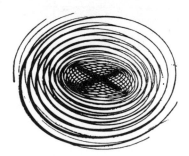

* For a medieval approach to this same question, see St. Bonaventure's " On Retracing the Arts to Theology, " Volume II, " The Works of Bonaventure, " translated from the Latin by José de Vinck, St. Anthony Guild Press, Paterson, N.J. 1966.

THE DIFFERENT LEVELS OF HUMAN DEVELOPMENT

AS LIFE goes on, the actual level of fulfillment of a man becomes clearly discernible : he may be arrested on the emotional, symbolical, or dogmatic level, or he may be free.

There are many adults in terms of age who for some reason or other have not managed to go as far as they could in the order of human perfection. Some of them live by emotional images and sensory impulses, obeying instinct rather than reason. They are truly overgrown infants. They react to the various circumstances of life with uncontroled greed or wild frustration, with elation or despair. They live in spurts of disorganized energy, or rather, of energy organized in a primitive way, considering only the most powerful urge of the moment. There is here little preplanning. Some measure of happiness may be obtained as long as all goes well, but there is pained amazement when it does not. Failure may then turn into brooding, a spirit of vengefulness and anti-social violence.

We all know of the overwhelming possession of an afflicted mind brought about by some great personal sorrow. The whole universe, the world of rational thought and emotional tension, is then reduced to one throbbing point of pain. Nothing else seems to exist—and the supreme insult is that the sun continues to rise joyfully over the dawn of our sorrow, in complete indifference to what is shattering us, and the same crowds rush to their daily task as if nothing had happened. This, in a sense, is the constant state of the primitive, the total bewilderment of the undeveloped, and a clear sign of childishness. The hard thing to admit is that in fact nothing has happened—to the outside world. And the wise thing to do is to grow up and rebuild our own crumbled world precisely with the elements of healthy indifference of the people around us.

On the second level are those who live in a mythological world through a personification of their value-system, remaining at an early stage of superstition, giving more credit to horoscopes or to their favorite devotion than to the message of life and love of the Gospels. These are the children of the symbolical, anthropomorphic age.

Others again cling to imaginary absolutes, remaining in a state of metaphysical triumphalism and providing simplistic and clear-cut solutions and answers that are often incompatible with the subtle and evolving mystery of the universe. They are the adolescents of the " age of reason. " They may be badly shaken by the evidence of disorder and pain in themselves and others. They are then tempted to retire within their ego and to invest their all in some future reward entirely disconnected from the too-terrible reality of the day. They are the absolutists who have developed for themselves a beautifully smooth theory of heaven and earth. They live by the rule, the law, the precise command of their clear conscience. They expect results to match their patterns of thought and have a tendency to impose their views on others and to conform them in Procrustean fashion to the supposedly good and right.

Authoritarian fathers and rulers are to be found here, and also the members of the Inquisition. They know all the answers. And even if these answers have resulted in a life of rigidity and isolation, they will see to it that the next generation will attain through these same rules the abstract perfection they themselves have failed to reach. Such minds are arrested on the metaphysical level. In spite of their immense good will, they are inflicting enormous harm upon their followers. Few people are more dangerous than a man of strong principles whose principles are not quite right.

The free people, the lovely people alone are true adults, able to rise to the level of acceptance of mystery, but also to the wisdom of acknowledging that, indeed, the world is good. This implies both clarity of vision as regards what can be seen, and admission of " the cloud of unknowing " as regards what cannot. Such a level of authenticity is attained only as a mystical and living state of union with reality, at the end of a course that implies considerable study and the gift of intuition which the religious-minded call the presence of the Holy Spirit.

The truly wise, who never were so smug as to believe in a well-ordered world they could fully understand and handle right here and now, have managed to survive quite well in the precariousness of the world as it is. They have developed a flexibility that should not be confused with laxism or defeatism : a laxist would have betrayed his inner faith, and a defeatist would have given up. The flexible person keeps applying pressure in the general direction of his well-determined goal so as to take advantage of any unexpected opening without ever being surprised by unexpected obstacles. Such men and women float with astonishing ease, towering over the waves of both catastrophe and triumph. They are fully conscious of their emotional and instinctive needs and are in full control of their thoughts. Instead of taking abstract principles as the rules of their life, they see them merely as props to reality, intellectual skeletons to be draped with the roundness, warmth and delight of living flesh. Their concern is not an other-worldly dream, but the mystery of the here and now. They approach every endeavor, even the most important, with a certain light-heartedness, a certain sense of humor that says, " Let's give it a good try. If I fail, I'll try again, or switch to something else. But as of now, I will give it my best. " This is not preplanned failure, but a realistic foresight that considers the possibility of failure and prepares a man to face it if it comes, while also leaving the door open to success.

Instead of believing they know all the answers, lovely people work out each necessary answer, slowly and carefully. They are often confused and sometimes wrong, but their errors are never mortal nor are their losses final. They are full of bounce, vitality, joy because of their adaptation to a world that is by nature an unfathomable composite of happiness and sorrow, success and failure, truth and error, evidence and mystery. And since their deepest desires are so closely related to the greatest mysteries—life and love—they proceed both cautiously and lightheartedly. Cautiously, because nothing is more important than life and love; lightheartedly, because once they have accepted the mystery and done all in their power to pierce it, they have nothing more to do than relax and enjoy whatever happiness comes their way.

These lovely people, then, will live with great respect for themselves and for others, since they perceive through active participation the community of all men of good will. They will meet beyond national, racial or religious boundaries in the confraternity of those who believe in the same truths and share the same dynamic but realistic optimism. They are the hope of the world, the foundation of the future Ecclesia, the first scattered elements of the union of all.

The notion of the complete self-sufficiency of any item of finite knowledge is the fundamental error of dogmatism.

ALFRED NORTH WITHEHEAD

I would wish to see a world in which education aimed at mental freedom rather than at imprisoning the minds of the young in a rigid armor of dogma calculated to protect them through life against the shafts of impartial evidence.

BERTRAND RUSSELL

The clash between science and religion has not shown that religion is false and science is true. It has shown that all systems of definition are relative to various purposes, and that none of them actually grasp reality. And because religion was being misused as a means for actually grasping and possessing the mystery of life, a certain measure of " debunking " was highly necessary. ALAN WATTS

We are thus in a position to distinguish two moments in the development of the Christian faith. The first moment is positive, and it consists in overcoming inevidence. The second is negative, and it consists in overcoming credulity... The Christian God is not both transcendent and immanent. He is a reality other than being (by which presence he makes being to be). LESLIE DEWART

CHAPTER 2

THE TEACHING
OF RELIGION

THE OLD AND THE NEW SCHOOLS

THE RIGHT UNDERSTANDING of love— love of God and love of men—will be available only to those who have reached the highest stage of human evolution. They alone will have a true notion of right and wrong and the ability to impart it properly. Only those who live as fully free and fully human beings will be qualified teachers of goodness, teachers of love.

Unfortunately, many people seem to know little about love, and to care even less. As far as they are concerned, it is useless for moralists to write about a refined conscience, the proper use of freedom, the value of ethical principles. They do not understand and are not interested because they are arrested on a sub-human, sub-ethical and sub-religious level. In fact, they often do not have a refined conscience, nor do they know or care how to use their freedom or how to find the proper rules of rightful living. Perhaps they do not even know they are free, since they act from moment to moment under the impulse of the most urgent need, restrained only by the prospect of immediately unpleasant consequences of their deeds. They do not use their rational powers in the determination of right and wrong, they do not think.

This is the situation of many young people. Can we blame them for it? They have been told repeatedly, " Do this! Don't do that!" by their elders who at the same time were indulging in what they prohibited in the young. Their religious education, if any, had often consisted in memorizing texts they did not understand and could not assimilate. They were seldom told about the mysteries of faith, the pain of believing, the burdens of temptation, darkness, doubt. Religion had been offered to them in neat and dry abstract formulas to be pulled out of storage and applied according to circumstances. As soon as they found out how seldom the rigid formulas matched the fluidity of life, they threw out the whole set like a stack of broken records and replaced it with the law of the jungle : " Grab as much as you can without getting too badly hurt." They had been taught by old-fashioned instructors who attempted to graft abstract spiritual teachings on the wild shoots of instinct without the intermediate development of personal discipline and the practice of the natural virtues of reason and prudence. In a gross oversimplification reminiscent of Platonism and Manicheism, they had been told that the soul was opposed to the body, the spirit to matter. Pie-in-the-sky had been promised to those who scorned the flesh and the world—and the distinction was seldom made between the world of wickedness, the kingdom of the Prince of Darkness, and the world of which God was pleased because it is good; between the flesh of lustful greed and that of the Incarnation.

Many are those who propagated and received this distorted view, who swallowed it whole and undigested and suffered blindly from its inadequacy to solve the major problems of life. Few things are more damaging than improperly checked belief handed down and accepted uncritically.

Happily, there is now a new school of religious teaching run by well-informed humanists and theologians who offer and practice an enlightened interpretation of the truth. They make men free, responsible, open to the breath of the Spirit, concerned with the neighbor's welfare. Their attitude combines great humility before the mysteries of faith with great confidence in the power of good will and the value of divine love. Their teaching imparts a deep sense of sorrow because Supreme Love is so little loved and so seldom understood. Many more people would now be believing Christians if they had been exposed to this kind of enlightened teaching.

One of the characteristics of the new school of religious teaching is a movement away from literal dogmatism and towards a more humble acceptance of mystery. In the metaphysical stage of religious training, there had been overemphasis on the importance of verbal expressions, on words rather than contents, on dogmatic formulas rather than on their mysterious objects. Strenuous attempts were being made towards ever-greater clarification, towards exhausting the mystery through the multiplicity of definitions, distinctions and sub-distinctions, by using methods of thought that were over-rationalistic. Religion had been made to consist essentially in the blind acceptance of a set of rules, creeds and rituals. The new school of religious teaching seeks to return to the truth behind the words, and in doing so it assumes a position of much greater humility that implies the constant presence of doubt. Even revealed truth does not have absolute validity in every one of its written expressions. This is due to the supreme dignity of the mind; nothing short of the face-to-face vision of Truth in person, God himself, can force our total assent. No amount of truth in the world has an absolutely determining power. Everything is a matter of balance and measure.

No intelligent man can be content to live without doubt, or rather, without overcoming through faith the gap that exists between the extreme reach of his intelligence and the fullness of reality. For man on earth, doubt is part of the very search for truth, and it will remain with us in some form or other until the end. That is why the rationalistic approach is a fallacy : a philosophy that makes of the human reason the limit and justification of the universe necessarily falls short of the mystery that is the universe. Yet, we do function as intelligent beings. Without making of reason the measure of the universe, we may use reason to the limit of our ability to penetrate as far as possible into the mystery. What little of it is accessible to our minds through revelation or intuition must be expressed through the conventional signs of language. But we must go further than language to discover at what precise point intelligence must give way to love and rational understanding to a blind Amen.

We will remain in a state of intolerable unrest until we have attained the source, reason and end of all things. Since all three are transcendent to the world itself, and human intelligence is part of the world, any contact with such matters must come about through means superior to the usual way of human understanding, that is, through intuition and inspiration : natural and supernatural grace.

No valid interpretation of the numinous, no religion, is possible without belief, which in turn must be expressed in the form of a dogmatic creed. But no verbal expressions can represent perfectly what is in fact not only beyond words but also beyond concepts. Dogmas are not the essential part of religion, but merely sign-posts, handrails, *garde-fous* (fool fences) as the French would say, that prevent our reason and thought from going completely astray. Dogmas have been elaborated through the ages by prophets and seers, systematized by theologians, confirmed by Church authorities. Yet no theological system can ever be the complete expression of the relations between man and God. Theodore L. Westow makes this point clearly :

> One may well ask whether theology and philosophy are sufficiently alive when they have been locked up in a closed system of abstractions. Perhaps theology and philosophy should not be looked upon as systems at all : but rather as supple, coherent, and harmonious interpretations of reality—and the justification of an interpretation should not be sought in whether it fits into an a priori established system, but whether it fits in with the harmonious correspondence of the rest of reality, on the same basis that the safest guide for the theologian lies in the harmony of the Redemption. *

At no level should adherence to *an expression* of faith be required as an absolute condition for membership in the Church, since all expressions that attempt to represent a mystery may be progressively refined and developed and filled out from inside. Certainty grows and wisdom increases from within, so that no wording of truth can ever be final and absolute. The error of the Inquisition is precisely to have enforced blind assent to verbal formulas. Erasmus of Rotterdam pointed out the danger of excessive dogmatism :

> In my opinion, many would be reconciled with the Roman Church in which all are now gathered as if in one herd, if we did not wish to define every little thing as if it were a matter of faith. It is enough that we rely on those things that are expressly stated in the Scriptures or constitute what is essential for salvation : these are few. The lesser the objects of faith, the greater will be the number of believers. At present, however, out of one object we make six hundred articles. Many of them could be omitted or doubted without any serious loss

* " The Variety of Catholic Attitudes, "

of devotion. The more definitions we pile up, the more we lay the foundations of dissent. The nature of mortals is such that once something has been established, they cling to it to the point of absurdity. *

A selection must be made constantly between the available definitions of religious truths. Perhaps some early and cherished beliefs will fall along the way, discarded as sentimental imagination or too human interpretation of the unknown. What remains is elevated, purified, weeded of accidentals and externals, reduced to the naked fact of our relationship with the Beyond... until this relationship itself is resolved in the simplicity of mystical love. At that point, the Beyond becomes the Within, the Transcendent becomes the Immanent, the very reason for the " I " in me, not only " the ground of our being" of Paul Tillich, but that by which the ground of our being exists and towards which we tend. Such is the proper pilgrimage of every man and woman along the way of conversion from dogmatic memorization to existential religion.

Dogmatic definitions and moral rules should be accepted only as potentially right. Conviction cannot be handed down : it must be earned, it must grow and develop within each individual. Dogmatic teaching alone is insufficient food, for the truth cannot be received ready-made : it must be worked out by each one of us. Every point of faith must acquire an existential value, a direct relevance to us, here and now, for religion is essentially a personal matter, personal reverence in the face of evidence that exceeds rational analysis, a surrender which is at the same time a victory because it acknowledges a liberating fact : we are not alone.

Faith in God does not consist in lowering oneself before some haughty oppressor from some other world : faith is an assent to a power so far superior to our own that this very assent brings us into a higher order of existence, delivering us from the slavery of non-being, absurdity, sub-human anguish and obsession.

* Letter to the Bohemian John Schlecta, 1519.

THE TEACHERS OF LOVE

LET US NOW take a look at the great teachers of love and religion from East and West and see whether they have any common traits that make them what they are. Two characteristics emerge at first sight from the lives of Socrates * and Aristotle, Confucius and Lao Tsu, the Buddha and Arjuna, Thomas Aquinas and Bonaventure, Francis of Assisi and John of the Cross and their more recent counterparts, and essentially, from the life of Christ : a strong measure of ascetical *discipline*, and intense *love* and concern for humanity. No great task is ever achieved without preliminary sacrifice, without dedication to something over and above immediate pleasure. It may be a lifetime of prayer, or one of silent study or active involvement in society; it may be spiritual contemplation or scientific research. In every instance, there is a stern, persistent, courageous effort, a focusing of energies upon a worth-while goal.

Self-interest is no such goal : the insignifiance of one's person compared to the scale of the universe makes of narcissism a joke and a disaster. When love expands to encompass the other, changing Sartre's hell into a potential heaven, the goal becomes commensurate with man's desire. Working for the love of man is working for the love of All—which is one of the names of God.

Besides discipline and love, a third characteristic may be found in the lives of the great teachers of goodness : *universality*. The words and deeds of the truly wise have a quality of timelessness that makes them part of the common treasury of mankind. Wisdom—and particularly the genius of wisdom—consists in the ability to draw out of the commonplace of life some creative truth that adds to the dimension of happiness of those who receive it.

But how can the lives of the great and the wise affect our own? We generally lack their gifts, and probably also their courage; we lack their early training, their habits of order and discipline, their concentration on some chosen aim. We are all too seldom

* Plato is omitted intentionally, since in spite of his genius, he had a very dubious understanding of human love.

concerned with such major subjects as our final destiny, the reason and end of the universe, the meaning of God. Yet, we do have some measure of intelligence and free will : intelligence enough to find out where we should be going, and free will enough to direct us precisely there.

Because of the metaphysical precariousness of our being, we are never set in a definite pattern as long as we live. The state of " being established in a definite pattern" is a very good definition of death. By our own merit or our own fault, we will at that time be set in an everlasting personal pattern every thread of which we are spinning and weaving right now through all the moral decisions, large or small, that make up our daily life. If this pattern is not reasonably preplanned, it may turn into a hideous jumble of false starts, disastrous defeats and worthless victories—and we may end up, not as lovers of all that is good, but as a sorry mess.

Whatever our present position, it is not final. Sinner may turn into saint and saint into sinner with astonishing speed. What we need in order to turn from thoughtless irresponsibility to wisdom and happiness is a clear determination of where we are going, and why, in the light of our deepest aspirations. The teachers of goodness will show us that it consists in doing what is right in terms of love, again and again, painfully at first, then with ever-greater ease as effort turns into habit, habit into wisdom, and wisdom into our natural way of life.

The danger is that the formation of habits works both ways. If our goal is too low, or, God forbid, actually evil, we will grow with ever-greater ease into the habit of imperfection or wickedness, the habit will turn into vice, and vice into the destructive way of death : satanic hatred.

Total happiness is unobtainable in a world limited by time and space. It is doubly impossible because we ourselves are in contact with such a small slice of this limited whole, while at the same time desiring the perfection of all. We can never be completely happy on earth, but we can be reasonably happy and completely at peace. No perfect happiness is possible as long as there is sin and suffering and death, for we all sin with the sinner, suffer with the suffering and die with everything that dies. Total happiness would imply the awareness that all is well here and now. What we have instead is a confused awareness of our immediate surroundings, much of which is quite wrong. But we are always able to strive towards right. We are either the builders or the destroyers of human perfection, both in ourselves and in others; we are all missionaries, teachers of love or hatred.

We finally turn to the Good Book, the ancient Bible, that fantastic aggregate of legend and history, brutal misconduct and deep wisdom; we consider its many commentaries, the mountains of religious writings it inspired, the works of the Fathers and the saints. At first, we may wonder how anyone could be so naive as to fall for such a jumble of obsolete or distorted traditions, human errors and pretense. Then, with the help of the gift of faith, through gratuitous grace, we look again and discover beneath the human imperfection the miraculous and patient action of the true God of Love.

God's coming down, real and subtantial, into intelligent nature, is a continuous and daily act.   AUGUSTE GRATRY

We are loved as powerfully as we are created.
                                        VLADIMIR GHIKA

We can say nothing true about God but he is not this, he is not that. Shall we therefore keep silent? God forbid! For he has bidden us to praise him. And I am quite perfectly certain that the ultimate truth of the created universe is that which is implied in the saying of Julian of Norwich : " It lasteth and ever shall, for God loveth it, " and that as the actuality of everything is dependent upon God's will, so everything is sustained in being by his love.   ERIC GILL

CHAPTER 3

THE BIBLE
AND THE CHURCH

HOW TO READ THE BIBLE

IN OUR IMPATIENT TIMES, there seems to be a general tendency to do away with the past, mistrust the wisdom of the ages, brush off all earlier belief and start again from scratch. This tendency seems characteristic of youth : it is both touching in that it reveals the wish for total perfection, and embarrassingly ineffective in that, as we have seen, it tends to reduce its follower to the level of the primitive by depriving him of the results and acquisitions of human progress. Traditional sources may contain an accumulation of useless and even damaging notions together with the flowers and fruits of wisdom. Yet, an overgrown orchard is considerably better than a desert : all it needs is some pruning before it can yield an abundance of food. A desert will take immense labor before it can be made to produce anything at all.

Let us then consider the most ancient and controversial book : the Bible. Between uncompromising Fundamentalism and total skepticism, there is the position of reason, and it consists in accepting the Good Book for what it is : not an absolute and definite catalogue of vicious or virtuous acts, not a complete formulary of moral solutions, not an object of such sanctity that it cannot suffer historical, literary, or exegetical criticism, but the work of a collection of immensely different authors, inspired by some mysterious power that exceeded their personal and limited abilities, resulting in a mixture of revelations from the deepest recesses of reality with a considerable amount of Jewish folklore and prejudice, and the visibly damaging effects of human imperfection, often in the form of appalling violence.

This may be seen clearly in much of the Old Testament with its unbelievably bloody and savage practices particularly in the treatment of conquered cities. Even the New Testament does not reflect perfectly the doctrine of pure love advocated and practiced by Christ. The composers or compilers of the Gospels necessarily saw him through their own human and limited intelligences. They made their own personal judgments as to which parts of his teachings were to be either mentioned or omitted. As close as the Gospels may be to representing the life and words of Christ, they are still a work of human art, and as such, imperfect. The same is true of the Epistles : a personality as strong as that of Paul of Tarsus necessarily comes through in his writings. Hence, a certain rigidity and anti-feminism that do not seem to accord with the Master's spirit.

The Bible, then, must be taken with a grain of salt. This does not exclude reverential awe before God's word, even if offered in a touchingly human form. Instead of rejecting the Bible on account of its imperfections, we should accept all that it has of good : the completely fascinating story of the covenant between God and man, the progressive development of this alliance of love, the lifting of man through man, most of all through the incarnate Christ.

If there is one thing that clearly comes from reading the Bible, it is a full awareness of the human condition. This implies the importance of the here and now, that is, the fact that the evolution of mankind is founded, not on pious thoughts of pie-in-the-sky, but on the down-to-earth, daily toil of living. *In much religious writing, other-worldliness has been separated erroneously from this-worldliness, as if it were enough to escape from life in order to attain Life. On the contrary, the Bible clearly shows that Life itself—the presence of God—is the most important factor of our presence on earth, the principle and sustainer of which is the Spirit of Love.*

The same concern for the present may be seen in Christ : he prepared a meal of bread and fish for his disciples on the shore, he nourished the multitude, he asked that they feed the daughter of the widow from Naim, he took food and drink in the meeting hall after his resurrection. Again, what is perhaps the foremost document of Christianism, the Sermon on the Mount, reads not at all like a manual of ascetical theology, but on the contrary, as a matter-of-fact imparting of advice of immediate existential import. The Beatitudes are not addressed by an other-wordly prophet to candidates for other-worldliness; the kingdom of heaven promised to the poor in spirit is within them, an uncluttering of the mind that opens it to the limitless possibilities of love. The meek shall possess the earth, by contrast with the violent who can only destroy it. Those who mourn will be comforted right now if their mourning is true, if they weep because Love is not loved and because man receives insufficient justice from his brothers. They will also find their reward if they not only mourn but act because of their hunger and thirst for justice. The merciful shall obtain mercy, as the man who lives by the sword shall die by the sword. The clean of heart shall see God because they have not pretented they owned him. The peacemakers shall be called children of God, the brothers of the Prince of Peace. Those who suffer for justice' sake shall enter the kingdom of heaven, the kingdom of an enlightened conscience where the Spirit of love is reigning—and the inimaginable kingdom of the Promise which" eye has not seen nor ear heard, nor has it entered the heart of man". All these beatitudes, these happinesses, belong right here and now, both in their prerequisites and their aftereffects. We are never left waiting.

How can the spirit of the Beatitudes be reawakened in the Church? Good Pope John originated the present movement when he proposed an *aggiornamento*—a bringing up to day—at the beginning of the Council. There is almost universal agreement as to the need for improvement in the Church, but much disagreement as to the proper means and goals. This may be due to general confusion as to the object in need of improvement : the Church itself. What in fact is the Church? A careful analysis of the widely different realities covered by the one term may help determine the scope and importance of future renewal.

WHAT IS THE CHURCH?

TAKING the term Church in its very highest meaning, it may be seen to designate the all-pure Bride of Christ, the community of worshipers in spirit and in truth. There is nothing here to renovate or reform. But such a Church is the Holy Jerusalem that has not yet come down from heaven. It is THE CHURCH OF THE PAROU-SIA (1).

— The Church is also that historical institution established by Christ that has come to us through direct apostolic succession. In that sense, the term applies to the CATHOLIC CHURCH (2), the ORTHODOX CHURCH (3), and to some of the higher Protestant Churches, Episcopalian, Lutheran, etc.

— The Church may also be understood as applying to a grouping of societies all of which claim Christ as their center. This is the CHRISTIAN CHURCH (4).

— The term may apply to the governing body in its hierarchical and administrative function. This is the INSTITUTIONAL CHURCH (5).

— Again, it may be a personification of the teaching authority conferred by Christ upon his apostles and their successors. This is the MAGISTERIAL CHURCH (6).

— Once more, it may apply to the communion of those who have given their allegiance to the true teachings of Christ, irrespective of lay or religious status : This is the true CHURCH OF THE COMMUNION OF SAINTS (7).

— Finally, the Church may be seen as consisting in the union of all those who live in the spirit of love, whether or not they belong to any Christian group. This is the MYSTICAL BODY OF CHRIST (8).

The Church of the Communion of Saints (7) and the Mystical Body of Christ (8) represent as much of the perfect Church as has been completed in our time. It is these two forms that are worthy of hymns of praise, for instance the German poet Gertrud von Le Fort's *Hymnen and die Kirche*—although they seem to be addressed rather to the Church under (7) than under (8). The Church that is very much in need of improvement is that covered by numbers (2) to (6) inclusively.

The Catholic Church (2), founded by Christ, governed by his Vicar assisted by the apostles' successors is a widespread religious, political, philosophical and economic complex administered from Rome and branching out throughout the world in the form of dioceses and parishes. *In one sense, it may be identified with that Church against which the gates of hell shall not prevail; in another sense, it may not. The guarantee of perpetuity, the protection of the Holy Spirit, the continued presence of Christ are assured to it as long as it coincides with the Communion of Saints (7), and not in every one of its enterprises.* Within the true Church of Christ, there are countless departments, human in both their personnel and their goal, whose errors, blunders, sins and even crimes have marked the course of history without destroying the Church itself since they were not identified with it. Many of these same departments are still with us, encumbered with too much wealth, too many outmoded traditions, too many prejudices, and the conservative bent of the Rich Old Man. But in its essence, this same Catholic Church still contains the fullest expression of Christ's message.

Almost the same may be said of the Orthodox Church (3).

The Christian Church (4) does not concern us here, since it is constituted by a grouping of individual Churches, and what we are concerned with here is the reformation of our own.

The Institutional Church (5) is of major importance in the present study. In the discussions that preceded the publishing of the Vatican II document *De Ecclesia*, two conflicting views appeared clearly : the conservative, which considered the Church as an organization of celibates whose authority dominated the mass of the faithful; and the progressive, which saw the Church as the mass of the faithful, served by some of their own endowed with priestly Orders. A considerable majority seems to have favored the latter view, yet the final text is a compromise.

The danger of the conservative view of the Church as an authoritarian organization is that it tends to dehumanization. In a highly centralized system, the trend will be to have everything of importance entrusted to organization men steeped in the system with its massive and insensitive unity. Such men would rather see the people crushed by the moloch than suffer any infringement of their rules. There is dehumanization on several levels : in the training of seminarians, the emphasis on buildings over human values, the enforcement of power structures over and above personal development and freedom of expression, the irreality of convent and rectory life where all material needs are abundantly and automatically provided by the faithful (at least in this country) and often spent with such lavish unconcern, without any sanction, control or responsibility.

The authoritarian system of Church government has been entrenched so solidly and so long that it is only through a rare concurrence of history and inspiration from above that such a freedom-loving spirit as Angelo Roncalli could ever have become Pope John XXIII and attained his position of world-wide influence. May his spirit remain forever in the Institutional Church to which he gave its first real chance in modern times to bring about many essential reforms. Clearly, the Institution should be for the people, and not the people for the Institution. But such a simple and obvious principle is not always applied.

As for the Magisterial Church (6), there is no doubt about the teaching authority of Pope and Bishops. But much more attention should be given to two elements : fully competent research on any level of authority before the publication of a decision; and respect for the sense of the people, the charismatic gift received by every baptized Christian that may give rise to a communal expression of belief, or to the very special messages of the prophet. In that sense, infallibility belongs to the Magisterial Church only insofar as its decisions are well-founded and represent the totality of the faithful. It is not the personal prerogative of an individual (the Pope alone) or of a group (the college of Bishops), but of the whole Ecclesia. It is against the *Church* that the gates of hell shall not prevail, not against *Peter*. The Church here is to be understood as the Communion of Saints (7).

As a case in point, the recent encyclical *Humanae vitae* is faulty for having disregarded the facts of human physiology and psychology, the opinion of the majority of the Special Papal Commission on Birth Control, and the sense of the people, in favor of an abstract and inhuman perfection. *The Magisterial Church is not the source of truth but only its mouthpiece. The only source of truth is Christ who speaks through whomsoever he pleases. If and when members of the hierarchy make dogmatic or moral decrees independently of the clearly expressed opinion of the faithful through whom the*

Spirit may be speaking, there is something lacking in their credibility.

The Church will act as the official agent of our communal worship, the visible sign of the practice of our religion. In spite of its imperfections, we cannot do without our Church. We should not destroy it and attempt to rebuild it from the ground up, out of some primitive zeal for perfection. With the gift of faith and through gratuitous grace, let us look at it kindly, realizing that it is ours and that its imperfections reflect our own. But let us also do our best to improve it and make it become what it should be, the glorious and indispensable Bride of Christ, our Holy Mother Church.

It is just because there is no-thing in the One that all things are from it.   PLOTINUS

God's remoteness is the incomprehensibility of his all-penetrating proximity.   KARL RAHNER

I shall declare now that which is to be known, by knowing which one attains immortality. The supreme Brahman is beginningless. It is said to be neither existence nor non-existence.
It exists within and without all beings; it is unmoving as well as moving, incomprehensible because of its subtlety; it is far and also near.
THE BLESSED LORD'S SONG (Hindu)

You have spoken to me enough for me to trust in your silence until death.   GUSTAVE THIBON

That which we can name is not God, for if men could understand him with their senses and their ideas, God would be less than they, and so we would soon cease to love him.
HADEWYCK OF ANTWERP

Zeus, whether thou art compulsion of nature or intelligence of mankind, to thee did I pray.   EURIPIDES

To the Unknown God!
DEDICATION OF AN ALTAR IN ATHENS

CHAPTER 4

THE MYSTERY
OF GOD

CAN MAN REACH GOD?

AFTER CONSIDERING MAN IN HIMSELF and in his relation to the Church, let us now turn our attention to the beginning and end of it all : God as he has made himself known to us. There is an inevitable margin between God as he is and God as man understands him. That is the fundamental reason why faith is so indispensable.

Many people have the arrogant tendency to believe they are the measure of the universe and even of its author. Anything they cannot understand they reject a priori, not only as an object of possible knowing, but even as an object of possible being. What they mean is : " I don't understand it, so it cannot possibly exist." At times, this attitude reduces belief to sensory experience. A positive scientist may deny the reality of anything that does not affect his instruments of measure. None but a Russian—that most religious of peoples and most atheistic—could have innocently and gleefully announced that he had not seen God in outer space. The nineteenth-century surgeon refused to believe in human spirituality because he had never found a soul under his scalpel. Many people declare, " There is no God" on the strength of the primitive reasoning that they have never met anyone who resembled the idea they have of him. Were the Son of God to walk again on earth, they would probably be the first to crucify him in the name of religion. Pilate could ask, " What is truth?" while Truth incarnate was staring him in the face.

The best theologian and deepest mystic cannot know God in any way commensurate with what he is. They know something of him, they do have some contact with him, rational for the theologian and existential for the mystic. But the first step in the search for God is the totally unashamed, humble and realistic attitude of the man who admits he doesn't understand.

The closest man ever came to God is expressed in the writings of the mystics, but whatever glimpse they perceived of his glory, they are unable to hand down to us. They weep at their own poverty of expression. In their apostolic zeal, they are eager to share their extra-vital, super-luminous experience of God with all God-hungry people. But when they get down to speaking or writing about it, hardly anything remains of the splendors they had seen.

When a diver in the glowing underwater world spots an azure-winged fish, a star of burning red, a purple and undulating anemone, his first thought is to pluck these marvels and show them to his friends. Alas, as soon as he passes from the water to the dry outer-world, all he has to show is a dying fragment of steel-colored flesh, a star of troubled pink, a shapeless ooze of grey...

The mystics are the divers of the spiritual world, living in a splendor that time and space cannot contain. When they rise to the surface of our everyday world, they hold but the extinct fragments of the glories they had seen. Let us believe, with the diver, that in all truth the fish was dazzling blue, the star incandescent red, and the anemone purple and graceful beyond words. And let us believe with the mystic that God is infinitely beautiful in an infinite variety of ways.

THE PROBLEM OF THE EXISTENCE OF GOD

THE FACT has been indicated above that the existence of God cannot be proved rationally. Let us now go a little deeper into the difficulty. Since God is beyond conceptual representation, trying to prove or disprove his existence is as much of a wasted effort as the pursuit of perpetual motion or of the squaring of the circle : there is in it an inner contradiction.

God may be seen as a postulate, a fact antecedent to any proof and upon which everything else must rest. Since everything depends upon him, nothing can serve as a proof of him. Either God is and does not need to be demonstrated, or he is not and cannot be demonstrated. He is the fundamental assumption, the first data of everything else. He is either total reality or total myth—and each one of us is called upon to make a choice between the two and to live in accordance with this choice. There may be greater risk in taking reality for myth than in taking myth for reality—a point clearly made by Pascal in his famous " wager. "

The trouble with God seems to be that he is not a conqueror. Had he made himself into a forceful, glorious, visible leader—a great public figure such as the Jews dreamed of, and as they hoped Christ would become on the day they strew his path with palms—many poor souls would have bowed before him in fear and reverence as they do before any manifestation of human might. But his power is too great to be perceived, his armies are unseen, his action is too respectful of human freedom, and he himself is so much not a man, so different from anything conceivable and imaginable, so completely outside the categories of thought—not as a foreigner living by different rules or customs, but as the essentially unknown, the other, the beyond—that many shrug him off as too impossible, too unreal to be worth considering in the plan of their everyday life.

By overlooking him, they revert to an inferior state of intelligence : the condition of natural, non-enlightened rationality that considers the mind as its own master and end. And since this mind is all too clearly imperfect both as a master and as an end, they live in a state of constant frustration and unrest, constant search for escape into something else, which is precisely the infinite they had refused to consider.

As long as the mind does not take the plunge into the suprarational, it will be condemned to whirling around in the squirrel-cage of self disgust. Not that self is disgusting, but that it is insufficient as an end-all and be-all of the human dream. The Nietzschean and Sartrean self-adorers necessarily end up hating themselves, as a self-inflicted punishment for having sought the absolute where there is none.

The important thing for us is to reassess the meaning of God, and the best way to do so seems to be the method of resourcing, of going back to the origins of religion.

Much of what has been believed about God assumed a symbolic form. The reason is, of course, that since God cannot be encompassed with words, he must be presented through a series of signs or approximations. These signs coincide with the level of development of each successive age of man.

The earliest traces of culture reveal that primitive man seems to have had a deep sense of the sacred. He lived in a world of mystery, in a bewildering succession of occurrences to which he could assign no clear cause. His power of observation developed long before his power of reasoning, so that, through lack of any plausible explanation, he attributed almost every event to something magic, holy or divine.

In its earliest form, the religious spirit of man seems to have addressed itself to the forces of nature. Ritualistic cult and practices referred to natural and obvious realities : the sun and moon, the cycle of the seasons, fire, water, fertility and so forth. All received divine homage : they were divinized.

For the agriculturally and astronomically minded Egyptians, the Godhead was seen to be present in many forms, principally in the sun and moon, the night and day, the river Nile, and in some powerful or mysterious beasts : the crocodile, the falcon, the cat.

At a later phase of intellectual evolution, the importance of the human person was recognized. The same forces of nature were then identified with superhuman personages, forming elaborate mythologies. No longer were natural events the object of religious cult in themselves; worship was now directed to their mythical impersonators. Such was the age of the Greek Zeus, Hera, Helios, Poseidon, Ghea, Aphrodite, Pluto, Ares, Dionysios, etc., and of their Latin counterparts, Jupiter, Juno (or Minerva), Apollo, Neptune, Cybele, Venus, Vulcan, Mars, Bacchus, etc.

Later, an age of greater sophistication replaced such childish anthropomorphism : the age of metaphysics. The lively and often naughty human gods disappeared, leaving the stage to intellectual concepts and abstract ideas, the supreme good, the uncaused cause, the pure act, the first mover, etc. This, too, was the work of the Greeks.

Concurrently, in India, both symbolism and rationalism seem to have combined in that the inhabitants of the Hindu pantheon, while assuming human form, are incarnations of ideas rather than of natural event, Brahman, Vishnu, Devi, Shiva, etc., standing for power, wisdom, feminity, life and death, etc.

In the meantime, God had revealed himself to his chosen people as the unnamable one, the I AM, the Lord, the God of Abraham, Isaac and Jacob, promising future revelations through a Messiah yet to come. And when the time was fulfilled, Jesus Christ, the Son of Mary, the Son of God, was born in Bethlehem of Juda, lived in retirement, and after three years of preaching in public, was crucified and died and rose again on the third day.

From the simple beginning of a group of poor fishermen, the Church grew to encompass an enormous body of faithful under the guidance of an institutional hierarchy. When came the time to elaborate a theology and a philosophy, the tenets of revelation pertaining to the Living God were expressed in terms borrowed from Greek philosophy. This culminated in the Scholastic syntheses of Thomas Aquinas, Bonaventure of Bagnorea and Duns Scotus, as still taught in most Catholic universities and seminaries.

The question, now, is to determine how much of the Living God is properly represented by Scholastic dogmatism. Theology is a living science, evolving before our very eyes. *God will always be well beyond any theology, and so it is both the privilege and the duty of each conscious generation to reassess the doctrines of earlier ages. We seem at present to be reaching a new phase : after passing through the natural, the symbolical, the mythological and the metaphysical ages, theology is assuming a new humility and entering the mystical age of " wise unknowing."*

Instead of resting content in the smugness of his thought, modern religious man returns, with full awareness of his limitations, to adoring the utterly unknown. Instead of giving homage to the omnipotent, omnipresent, omniscient Great Spirit—an extension of human powers to the Nth degree— he bows in full consciousness of his ignorance before God, whatever or whoever he may be.

Primitive man had faced mystery everywhere, and worshiped it. Modern man has solved many mysteries, but as we have seen in the study of modern science, he is as far as ever from resolving the last. At the end of every avenue of research, he encounters an unlimited openness, a residue that escapes his grasp. It may be seen as a trace of God in the universe at that point where intelligence is forced either to revolt or to adore.

Man has now come full circle, from mystery to mystery. He knows what he knows, but is becoming ever more aware of his ignorance. He sees God " through a mirror, darkly, " as St. Paul puts it, referring to the roughly polished metal mirrors of his time. He lives in a cloud of unknowing, and is much the wiser for not pretending he understands everything. Yet, he is not an orphan living in the dark night of despair, for he is the son of the Father, the brother of Christ and the beloved of the Spirit. The mystery remains in full, but through revelation and the historical fact of a new mystery, the incarnation of Christ, and through the folly of the cross more mysterious perhaps than anything else, he knows where he stands and what he must do, for it has been spelled out for him in the Gospels.

The Scholastic, abstract expression of the mystery of God should not be discarded, but seen as a phase in the evolution of theological understanding. It may serve as a rich field for meditation and prayer. Its scope and value will be understood by considering the text of Bonaventure of Bagnorea offered in Appendix, p. 193.

Let us see, now, what can be said of God in terms of contemporary thought. The error of ancient philosophies consisted in believing that anything related to the Godhead could be defined. This resulted in giving the name of God to creations of the mind. Anything we are able to conceive necessarily falls short of the God we seek. Therefore what we seek is beyond conceptual thought. Nothing we are able to conceive can last forever. Therefore what we seek is independent of time. Nothing we are able to conceive is immense enough. Therefore what we seek is independent of space.

What we seek is not " up there, " nor is it " down here, " nor even " within, " and even less " without, " for in the latter case it would be inaccessible and we could not even think about it at all. The God we seek, then, is not only beyond the senses and imagination, but also beyond comprehension, and yet he is more real, more intimate to us than we are to ourselves.

Many valid theological views contain some insight into God's evermoving whole, but they serve only as artificial frames placing permeable boundaries around some fluid aspect of him. A system of theology may be seen as a basket plunged into the ocean. The basket itself has a clear and logical organization well within the capacity of understanding of the human mind. It does contain some of the ocean. What it holds may be analyzed in terms of temperature, salinity, plancton content, etc. But does the basket define and contain the ocean? The water is constantly flowing through the open weave, and the quantity of water contained and observed is immensely less than the ocean itself. As we have seen, the trouble with conservative, rationalistic theologians is that they take the basket for the ocean, the system of reference for the object studied, the theological definition for God himself. They tend to make absolutes out of a man-made mental structure which by its very nature is unable to contain the infinity of its object.

God does not even fall within the division of subject and object. If he did, he would either be a subject distinct from the objects he creates, or an object distinct from the subjects considering him. In both cases, there would exist some kind of being outside of him. There would then be two realities, God *and* his universe, and God could not be all since he would be ontologically distinct from the reality of his world. God is more subjective, closer to me than my own person, while at the same time he is so objective, so other, as to be the very reason and support of my existence. He is the objective source of my subjectivity, and the subjective source of my objectivity. The relationship is so subtle and so much beyond logically certain reasoning that it cannot be understood in full.

This notion is clearly expressed by Paul Tillich : " If the idea of God (and the symbols applied to him) which express man's ultimate concern is transferred to the horizontal plane, God becomes a being among others whose existence or non-existence is a matter of inquiry. " *

God belongs to an order distinct even from that of metaphysics, since " being" is a man-made concept. There are no two realities, the " being" of God and the " being" of creatures, but only one which includes both. *The nature of God comprises both himself and the power of bringing forth creatures, not as something distinct from himself, but as a mysterious element of his unicity. To the One-in-Three, creation of contingent beings is not a change nor a multiplication or extension of himself, nor a loss, but an actual aspect of himself. God could not not create without violating his self-diffusive nature. The power of the Father expressed by the Son through the life-giving love of the Spirit freely results in the creation of beings endowed with the power to express their love in the single act of living-loving.*

* " The Lost Dimension in Religion," in " Adventure of the Mind; " Vintage Book, N.Y. 1960, p. 57.

" God is dead. " Nietzsche
" Nietzsche is dead. " God   A GRAFFITI CLASSIC
God does not die on the way when we cease to believe in a
personal deity, but we die on the way when our lives cease
to be illumined by the steady radiance, renewed daily, of a
wonder, the source of which is beyond all reason.

DAG HAMMARSKJÖLD

Adolescents can no longer believe in their god, the god of
their system, the god of Fellini's Giulietta " behind the
trap door covered with dust over the stage of the convent
school. " They can hold on to that god for a long while
but when the door is finally thrown open they find neither
god nor a ravaging spider but instead emptiness or open
fields. Their utter amazement, confusion and despair at
this absence spring partly from two faults of ours : a) the
mythical picture that all children have of God has been
re-enforced in every detail by teachers who thought they
were building up a religious life; b) what is worse is that
when this picture begins to disintegrate as it surely must
in our modern world we do not rejoice with them and urge
them forward, but we try to make them return to childhood
when in fact they have nothing to go back to.

GABRIEL MORAN

He who thinks God is not comprehended, by him God
is comprehended; but he who thinks God is comprehended
knows him not. God is unknown to those who know him,
and is known to those who do not know him at all.

THE UPANISHADS

Words can be formed, concepts can be expressed, but man
cannot by his own effort reach God. The most he can hope
for is to receive a certain understanding which reveals
to him that God is mystery. But love lifts the veil.

CATHERINE DE VINCK

CHAPTER 5

THE DEATH
OF GOD

ORIGIN OF THE NOTION

WE ARE NOW in a better position to consider the Death of God movement. It seems to have had its origin in the pompous rhetoric of a German philosopher so inflated with grandiloquent pride that he ended in insanity. Friedrich Nietzsche (1844-1900), who may also be considered as one of the fathers of Nazi racism, announced to the world that God was dead, that he had actually come to an end within our historical time. The impact of this startling declaration was little more than that of a literary paradox which it actually was.

For this notion to be taken seriously, we must wait for our own time, when several authors revived the paradox, the best known of which is the Bishop of Woolwich, author of the book " Honest to God" which launched the great debate.

The major point Bishop Robinson attempts to make is that the notion of a God " up there" or " out there"—a being so unreal that it may be seen as dead—should be replaced with the notion of God " within" on the basis of Tillich's idea of the " ground of our being." The trouble, however, is that this still *places* God, attributing to him spatio-temporal characteristics which are no real improvement over earlier views. The theologians of the Death of God movement seem unable to admit the existence of an order of being that does not suffer any scattering in extension and duration, nor can they approach God through any method other than extrapolation of human ideas. Since this method is imperfect a priori, their results are inconclusive. Instead of blaming their faulty methods, they tend to deny the existence of a personal God. Because the extrapolation of the quality of human personality to the Nth degree does not fit God, they say that God is not a person.

In so doing, they are twice at fault : first, because they place God in the same ontological class as man, that is, in the order of "being," whereas the very notion of being is man-made and meaningless when applied to God. Second, because no amount of human understanding can comprehend in full the notion of personhood.

The notion of a personal God would not encounter any obstacle if it were approached from the viewpoint of negative theology, the only one that can apply properly to him. *God is not unpersonal*, that is, he has nothing of the imperfections and limitations of those beings that are below the personal level. Yet, we cannot say that he is personal or a person. No adjectival qualifier applies to him because of his unqualified unicity. The only truth we may securely assert of God is in the form of a denial of imperfections—and even the denial of perfections insofar as they are limiting qualifiers. However, we may say of God that he is subsistent as opposed to contingent, because subsistent is a negative in disguise : all that it actually means is non-contingent.

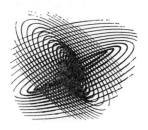

THE TRUTH ABOUT THE DEATH OF GOD

IN OUR exciting and forward-looking times, thoughts range from exhilaration over fresh discoveries to despair at the sight of crumbling faith. A few minds are challenged and passionately interested; many more are deeply disturbed because they feel the foundations of traditional beliefs are being destroyed. Their reaction is that of the little boy who prayed : "Dear God, take good care of yourself, for if anything happens to you, we are all sunk!" They themselves do not seem to have quite enough faith to be sure that nothing will happen to God. Some of them even suspect the worst : that God is not away on a trip, or sick, or wounded, but that he is actually laid out on his back with his mouth open like a fallen giant. Like Lazarus, *iam foetet*. The feeling is one of utter abandonment. Humanity has lost its Father and is now left to its own folly : the prospect of self-inflicted thermo-nuclear annihilation.

Is it true that at one time God existed as we knew him, but that he has died recently and can no longer be relied upon as the supreme provider of love and justice? Does it mean there is no longer any next world, and that Catholicism and every other religion are based on mere dreams, creations of the mind which this same mind now chooses to erase? Is our Father in heaven a myth, and are we now orphans reduced to the absurdity of waiting for Godot? Such is the conclusion of atheistic existentialism, the philosophy of despair. But it is not the truth.

God is dead, indeed, but not the Living God, the revealed trinitarian God of the mystics, the Lover of mankind, Father, Son and Holy Spirit. *The " death of God" means simply this : in the course of ages, by dint of reasoning and philosophizing, men have built for themselves an idol, an image of God, an imagination of God, a concept of God made to their likeness, accessible to their intelligence, encompassed by their definitions. They have done this in formal disobedience to one of God's sternest commands : " Thou shalt not make graven images."* They believe they have seen God and located him : he is an old man with a long beard seated on a throne somewhere beyond the clouds, condemning and rewarding men with the accuracy of a certified public accountant, according to the strict rules of his own system of sins, mortal and venial. Such is the popular image of God.

The more sophisticated have made another graven image. They too have seen him, but through metaphysical concepts as the Supreme Being of the Greeks. They have analyzed his attributes, scrutinized his powers, encompassed his nature. They have offered him to the adoration of the masses as a neatly packaged and fully satisfying concept. Too often, also, the image of God has been made of blown-up fragments of human power, with attributes and activities unworthy of him.

It is all these false images that are dying, these idols that are falling, and we may rejoice and do our best to hasten the day of our deliverance from them, of our return to God adored in spirit and in truth. The God whose death we may celebrate with joy is the conceptual God, the man-made idea of the Superman-plus, the God of wrath and vengeance, the Puppeteer pulling the strings of destiny in a capricious or absurd way, the thundering, cloud-born and peevish Zeus, the proper and puritanical God always ashamed at the sight of his naked children making love, the heavenly Potentate delighted with the pomp and glory of the Establishment, the Accountant of Indulgences.

If such a God is dead, alleluia! What a relief! A God with such feet of clay and such a face of deceit was bound to fall. With him come tumbling down mountains of false and sentimental piety, forests of dark and tangled anxiety, altars of gilt marble, vestments of embroidered scarlet and purple, all the sham and pretense of an earthly court, all the resounding and hollow halls of the Institution, all that is a scandal not only to the poor and simple-minded, but to all those who see the Church as the Bride of Christ, and him crucified, and who weep because there is still in her so much of the great Babylon.

Such is the God that is now dead. He is dead because he was never alive, nor was he ever God, but a mere man-made thing. Over and above classical definitions that futilely attempt to capture him, God may be found in an act of faith and love. He may be seen in the struggle of so many men and women of good will against vice, poverty, ignorance, war; in the silent forbearance or courageous efforts of the oppressed, the brow-beaten, the falsely indoctrinated who refuse to bow before a formula but seek the God of love as he truly is.

There was once a great Roman orator with a single-track mind. * He spoke often and powerfully of many things. But whatever his subject, his conclusion was always the same : " And furthermore, I feel we should smash Carthage." This came time and again, in season and out of season, but with such persuasive force that the Romans, as sensitive to a strongly worded slogan as any modern American, did go out and smash Carthage.

This seems to have little to do with the love of God, but there is a point to the story. When we read books and articles about God, we often have the feeling of being smothered in details. It is all so complicated, so involved, so obscure, so painfully criss-crossed

* Cato the Censor, 234-149 BC.

with distinctions, divisions and subdivisions. We are groping in a maze and end up greatly disappointed, for we were seeking God and find but the imperfect subtleties of human reasoning. Theology, however, is a good thing and all theologians should not be condemned automatically to a hell—or at least a purgatory—of torturing terms and concepts that always fall short of their goal. Let us be charitable and confess that theologians even have a right to heaven, but their chances would be greatly improved if they fed to their readers the Bread of Life instead of stones, the truth instead of subtle abstractions. But if in their incorrigible urge toward complication they cannot be content with writing a book that would repeat a million times over : GOD IS LOVE, AND THAT IS THAT—if, I mean, they feel the compulsion to write five hundred pages when ten would have done a better job, let them at least conclude every paragraph with the words Thomas Aquinas placed at the end of his monumental work : " All this is but straw, " and add again and again, " For God is love! "

GOD IS LOVE

SO MANY things have been said and written about love and so much vagueness and confusion are attached to it that some clarification seems indispensable.

In the most common meaning, " I love this music, this book, this girl, " the word refers to subjective attraction exercised by a desirable object. Love expresses our desire for a pleasurable good. The moral value of love will depend upon the suitability of the good in relation to our final end, which is the vision of God face to face. In simple words, love will be good as long as its object leads us to God.

It is possible and important to consider love, not only as subjective affection, but also in its objective truth. *Love is not only our desire for something : it is also a reality, a force, the supreme original, actual and final principle of all being.*

Love is the *supreme original principle of all being*. Love is identified with God and is the only reason for the creation of the universe, including man. Love is self-diffusive. Love has a tendency to expand beyond its own self. In the case of the supreme love, which is God, such expansion took the form of the Trinity, and of created beings within whom love could be multiplied and by whom it could be returned in a limited yet magnificent way.

Love is the *supreme actual principle of all being*. Everything that is partakes of love. The dignity of creatures, their level of honorability, depends upon their capacity to love and be loved. The more loving and lovable, the higher they are in rank. All things are real and existent in the measure in which they reflect love. They destroy their dignity when, abusing their freedom, they refuse to love. Redeemed man enlightened by revelation and empowered by grace is able to be loved infinitely and to love forever in return.

Love is the *supreme final principle of all being*. The final principle of a thing is also the first and original reason why it was made, its pre-planned purpose. To quote Thomas Aquinas, it is " first in the order of intention and last in the order of execution. " Nothing is ever made for nothing. If it was made at all, it is because it was foreseen for some purpose : but this purpose is fulfilled only at the end, when all is done. The final reason why all things were made is that love which is God. Nothing can be conceived independently of God, and hence, of love. Inferior creatures in the material universe came to be for the sole reason of glorifying God in an act of love, by being themselves, or being used by man on his way to God. And man was made, as every child of the Church is told, " to serve and love God and be happy with him forever in heaven. "

To summarize : everything that ever is *begins* because of love; everything that ever is *exists* through love; everything that ever is *tends* toward love.

The senses are innocent : self-deception is the work of thought and imagination. ALAN WATTS

O death, where is thy victory? O death, where is thy sting? PAUL OF TARSUS

No individual comes into the world as a sinner. Fashioned in the image of God, the creature is from his first hour surrounded by God's fatherly love. Consequently it is not true to say, as is often maintained, that the creature at birth is an enemy of God and a child of God's wrath. On the contrary, man becomes a sinner only through his own individual and responsible action. Nevertheless the creature who is born in the new covenant of time does not automatically share in the divine life of the risen Saviour. All creatures are called to this life, but they receive it only when they become united to Christ and become one with him as the branches with the vine.... Baptism does not effect the removal of " original sin, " but rather rebirth as a child of God. JOHN A. O'BRIEN

CHAPTER 6

THE PROBLEM OF EVIL
AND ORIGINAL SIN

A CRITICAL APPRAISAL OF CLASSICAL VIEWS

IF THE ONLY REALITY IS LOVE, how about evil, sin and death? They, too, seem real enough. How can they fit into the logical creation of a God of love? If there is a God and this God is perfect goodness, how can we explain the suffering of the innocent, war, disease and the countless other scourges that afflict mankind? Such things cannot be overlooked : hunger and suffering cry out too loud, war is present in our own sons, the flesh of our flesh and the hope of our hopes. Anyone who refuses to face such realities as these and to help alleviate the common burden is unworthy of humanity. But how can all this be reconciled with a God of love?

Every man comes unspoiled and young into a world that has been going on for so long that it seems damaged and old. Not that sunrise and ocean wave, mountain and meadow are any less good than they were millions of years ago, but that the dreary repetition and contagion of the unclean, the insufficient, the mean and the vicious has spread a shroud of decay over everything man touches. It is in this decayed world, however, that the young of man are born, and in this same world they often die before having achieved their own transcendence : their second birth and rational conversion.

Sin is generally considered under two general headings, original and actual. Original sin is the sin of Adam which, according to classical theology, is handed down to every man at birth. Actual sin is any evil act originated by the individual.

Is original sin a matter of dogmatic obligatory belief for the practicing Catholic? Although it is included quite forcefully in such summaries of Christian doctrine as the Baltimore Catechism, *

---

* "A Catechism of Christian Doctrine," St. Anthony Guild Press, Paterson, N.J. 1961, qq. 55 to 62.

there is now serious doubt about the validity of traditional teachings on the subject. Let us consider whether these teachings have any sriptural support. Thomas Aquinas, in the *Summa contra gentiles* indicates that original sin is handed down by our first parents to posterity :

> " 'Thou shalt die the death' (Gen. 2 : 17)—Now there would be no purpose in saying this if a man were created with the necessity of dying. Consequently we must say that death and the necessity of dying are a punishment inflicted upon man from sin. Now a punishment is not inflicted except upon those who are guilty. Therefore in all who are thus punished there must be some guilt.
>
> " ' Behold, I was conceived in iniquities, and in sins did my mother conceive me ' (Ps. 50 : 7).
>
> " ' Who can make him clean who is conceived of unclean seed? Is it not Thou who alone art? ' (Job, 14 : 4).
>
> " ' We were by nature children of wrath ' (Eph. 2 : 3). "

At first sight, these texts seem to defend the traditional thesis impressively. In fact, they are generally irrelevant. The quotation from Genesis is incomplete. What the full text says is this : " The day you shall eat of it you shall certainly die. " (And not, " you must die, " as in the CCD translation.) Both the Vulgate and the Septuagint may be translated, " On whatever day you eat of it, you shall die of death. " It would be completely illogical to draw from the complete text the notion that man was not liable to death before the fall, since the only thing implied is that as soon as man eats he will die. But since Adam ate of the fruit and remained physically alive, the word death must necessarily refer to spiritual or moral death, the loss of God's favor. This is clearly confirmed by the ensuing event, the expulsion from the Garden of Eden. If God had spoken of physical death, had threatened physical death to be triggered by the eating of the fruit, the fact that Adam and Eve ate of the fruit and did not die would prove God a fool!

In order to prove actual guilt, Aquinas quotes a number of other biblical texts which in his mind confirm an initial hostility toward God, a first sinful act at the very beginning of human life. This same idea will be used later by Church writers to develop a negative and erroneous theology of sex and marriage.

" Behold, I was conceived in iniquities, and in sins did my mother conceive me" (Ps. 50 : 7). A recent interpretation offered by the French " Bible de Jérusalem" reads in translation : " Behold, I was born wicked; my mother conceived me a sinner." The defect is clearly not in the mother's act, nor is it transmitted to the offspring as a guilty inheritance. The meaning of the text is simply that man is born imperfect and liable to sin, which is true. The two points Aquinas wished to make—guilt on the part of the mother and its handing down to the offspring—are not made at all.

" Who can make him clean who is conceived of unclean seed? Is it not Thou who alone art?" (Job, 14 : 4). Again, the " Bible de Jérusalem" has an entirely different interpretation : " But who indeed will extract the pure from the impure? No one." The text is completley irrclevant.

" We were by nature children of wrath" (Eph. 2 : 3). Once more, the " Bible de Jérusalem" interpretation disagrees : " We were by nature given to anger just like the others." The French has *voués à la colère*, which does not clearly indicate whether anger is that of God or that of man. If it is that of God, the preceding text clearly indicates that God's anger is brought about, not by any fault in our parents, but by our own faults. If it is man's anger, this confirms the thesis which will be developed later, that *original sin consists in a propensity to satisfy passions immediately, a remnant of the impatient and violent animal condition that must be overcome through grace*. In the second, subjective, interpretation, anger describes very well the loss of rational and spiritual control, the fall to a sub-human level. The phrase " just like the others" confirms that this is the common lot.

And so, none of the texts quoted by Aquinas in support of the idea of parental guilt transmitted to the offspring has the slightest relevance to his thesis, which is left up in the air as a figment of the theological imagination.

God's enmity is not incurred automatically : " original sin" is merely a sign, a remnant of an earlier and lower stage of evolution out of which we have not yet managed to move completely. It corresponds to our present condition, without implying any moral guilt on our part. We are as little responsible for our basic instincts as we are for having been born in the twentieth century rather than in the days of Julius Caesar or the cavemen. God's enmity can be brought about only by the actual, willful and personal sin of the Adam and Eve in us. And the punishment for such a sin is not the liability to physical death, which was always with us as part of our nature, but the immediate execution of spiritual death, the loss of God's grace and friendship.

There is in Genesis another passage that may be interpreted in the same sense. After the fall, God said : " And now perhaps he (man) will put forth his hand and take also from the tree of life and eat and live forever" (Gen. 3 : 22). How did the ancient comment-ators not see that, according to their interpretation, man did not need to touch the tree of life in order to live forever, since in their opinion he was not submitted to death anyway? If, on the other hand, man had been liable to death before the fall, as is evident enough, living forever would indeed have been a radical change which God, apparently, did not want. The tree of life in the midst of the garden has generally been identified with Christ. In that light, " eating of tree of life" may have symbolized the Eucharist—which in no way relieved man of physical death, but certainly contributes to his eternal life. God's prohibition could be seen as an indication that the time was not ripe for the coming of Christ and for the Eucharist. *

The natural state of man before the fall does not include immor-tality or deathlessness, but the innocence of irrational, non-free animality. The " peaceable kingdom" is a naive evocation of a dream that never existed : the world before the fall was without sin, but not without violence.

The principal objection to the integration of Genesis with scien-tific evolution disappears. Man did not come forth fully perfect on the face of the earth : he always was liable to death together with every other animal. The effect and meaning of the fall are in an entirely different order.

The state of natural perfection, before the fall, before the advent of conscious freedom and the liability of sin, consisted in the irres-ponsible, sinless, instinctual condition of the higher animal. The state of paradise may then be seen as that point of evolution at which man, at the dawn of intelligence and judgment, had not as yet

* A learned theologian, whose opinion I respect, informs me that this interpretation is " pure fancy." Under the circumstances, I offer it for whatever it is worth!

abused these powers by subjecting them to lower greed. Concupiscence, which classical theology associates with death as a second consequence of original sin, consists then in an instinctual remnant : the tendency toward immediate satisfaction of any affective desire, for food, warmth, sex, power, etc. The " old man" of St. Paul is a slave to such a condition, and the fall—of Adam and Eve in us, with the exception of Christ and his Mother—is that act by which, although elevated to the possibility of rational moral choice, we deliberately return to an inferior state, preferring our own will to that of God. By eating the " fruit," we become our own end, we " know" good and evil by claiming the power to determine right and wrong without any consideration for God's commands.

Original sin, then, did not introduce physical death into the world, but only death to grace. It consisted in the fact of man defying God. There is no universal original sin committed by our first parents and handed down by them. Infants cannot be guilty of sin because they lack the conditions of awareness and freedom. What they inherit is not sin, but concupiscence understood as a remnant of instinctual greed. *Adam and Eve should be seen, not as the original couple from which we all descend and receive an original stain, but as a valid symbol of every man and woman born into this world. It makes no theological difference whether man descend from a single couple or from many who followed parallel lines of evolution. In every instance, man displays in his personal evolution the characteristics of his symbol, Adam, and woman, those of hers, Eve.*

Adam represents evolution perceived at the moment of origination of intelligence and moral freedom. This moment cannot be pinpointed on any time chart, for it is the result of imperceptible progression. There is no need to imagine an evolutionary " leap" that would coincide with the instant of creation of the first soul, as there is no such leap in the development of an individual human being. The soul is not distinct from the being : it is the being insofar as it is able to act spiritually.

How did *homo sapiens* actually begin? Was he the object of a distinct act of creation in the sense that God waited for a few billion years for the earth to cool off, vegetation to grow, animals to develop, and then selected a particularly well formed pair of apes and injected souls into them? This seems as improbable as any other literal understanding of the symbolical elements of the Bible.

What then could have happened? Recent discoveries of paleontology indicate that thinking man is considerably more ancient than
anyone believed even fifty years ago. Instead of going back a few
thousand years as the Bible suggests, man is seen as an erect,
tool-using mammal at a time so distant from us that it boggles
the imagination. Instead of providing the legendary " missing
links," modern paleontology seems to show not only that these
links are too far in the past to be discoverable, but that they probably never existed at all. Teilhard de Chardin made the point
several times that the particular origin of any phylum—that is,
of any major evolutionary branch—cannot be determined, for such a
phylum can be known only after a large number of individual
members have left sufficient traces of their existence to be discoverable. There may also have been such a progressive mutation
that one stage could not have been distinguished from the next
because of the continuity of the process. Teilhard de Chardin
proposed the general principles of cerebralization, interiorization
and complexification—summarized as hominization—as a tendency
of the created universe in the act of developing its most promising
branch which eventually flowered into intelligent, God-seeking
man.

Every man coming into the world passes, as we have seen,
through every stage of the development of life. He is born an infant,
that is, speechless and incapable of rational thought. It is only much
later in life that it comes to resemble his Adam or Eve symbol. In
the infant, there is no sin, original or other, only a potential freedom.
This become actual sin, and merit become possible, only after reason
and free will have been developed sufficiently to take command.

If Adam's sin may be seen as a reversal to a lower state, may we
not find the same phenomenon in every man, at least as a propensity? Do we not, all of us, reach many occasions in life when the
choice is clearly laid before us either to grasp the immediately
profitable or to act in a way that implies restraint, generosity,
self-sacrifice and love for the neighbor? In that sense, all sons of
Adam and all daughters of Eve do suffer the consequences of
concupiscence. Baptism, then, is a visible sign by which the grace
of Christ is infused into a human being so as to make it a " new
creation," able to overcome the liabilities of an imperfect race.

And what is the action of the devil as regards the fall? There
is no reason to deny his existence : there are extremely powerful

spirits beyond the range of scientific instruments of detection. It is not because we cannot see them that they do not exist. It is, in fact, much safer to assume they do than to pretend they do not. The devil, whose brightest stroke of genius is to have made modern man believe he is a myth, is very much among us, perceptible in deeds of crime and horror and sheer evil that exceed human imagination. Evil is alive and active in many ways. There is, then, no foolish credulity in accepting much of the biblical story : the devil, Lucifer, the Prince of Darkness, the Fallen Angel becoming jealous of man on the brink of his birth to rational and spiritual life. Now that man has become capable of God and conscious of eternal bliss, by a subtle temptation, the evil spirit suggests the possibility of a return to a more satisfying because less responsible state : instinctive animality. He suggests at the same time a possible ascent to an entirely new state : competition with God. Every man, then, is tempted to re-enact the fall in himself. He is more liable to this than if Lucifer had not fallen : otherwise he would not have been so strongly tempted. But the grace of Christ received at baptism more than makes up for the power of evil, thus giving the man of good will a chance to choose right and avoid wrong. He needs constant help which he receives through constant grace, but he cannot rely on baptism alone : gratuitous grace demands a gratuitous response. In order to overcome the liability of original sin, understood as instinctive concupiscence, he needs the additional support of the Spirit of Life and Love, the Holy Spirit of God to whose breath he must always remain open.

EVIL AND FINAL JUSTICE

IT NOW remains to be seen how the presence of evil in the world may be reconciled with an all-good God. From what was said above, the conclusion may be reached that evil is a consequence of freedom. Freedom, in turn, is a condition of merit, and merit is the door to eternal happiness. Not that any deed of ours would give us any right to it, but that living meritorious lives as children of light makes us children of God who is love.

Without freedom, we could not get anywhere beyond the limits of our present reality. A creature whose actions are determined is neither good nor bad, but merely passive and morally indifferent. The possibility of choice, of positive action on the part of a creature that starts out in an imperfect condition necessarily entails the possibility of a wrong choice and failure. Moral or physical evil are the consequences of moral or physical failures on the part of imperfect creatures in the course of their voyage on earth. These evils, however, are never absolute. The only absolute evil is above the earth and consists in the loss of God. Many a form of hardship, many a physical or moral pain may serve as the occasion of acts of courage, affirmations of faith in the midst of adversities, of love in the face of hatred, of hope when all seems desperately dark. It is often then that God is the closest, as in the dark night of the spirit when he seems gone forever. It is of such sustained faith, hope and love in the face of every odds that man's final perfection is made.

The classical explanation to the problem of evil since Augustine consists in the notion that all will be well in the end, and that perfect order will be restored through appropriate reward and punishment. The explanation is still valid. Considered, however, in the light of daily occurrences, it may seem simplistic and over-optimistic. Yet, we should realize that all we see is a minute fragment of an immense whole which we are completely unable to comprehend. It is in God's own perspective, beyond the power of our concepts or imagination, that " all manner of things shall be well. " Our only task at present is to make things as well as we can in our own tiny corner of it all.

* Dame Julian of Norwich, quoted by T.S. Eliot in " Four Quartets. "

It is possible, and authentic wise men have proved that it is possible, to live in so large a world that the vexations of daily life come to feel trivial and that the purposes which stir our deeper emotions take on something of the immensity of our cosmic contemplations.
BERTRAND RUSSELL

There is in all men a demand for the superlative, so much so that the poor devil who has no other way of reaching it attains it by getting drunk. OLIVER WENDELL HOLMES

Man is not completed—that is the secret of his paradoxical behavior. LOREN EISELEY

I have one longing only : to grasp what is hidden behind appearances, to ferret out that mystery which brings me to birth and then kills me, to discover if behind the visible and unceasing stream of the world an invisible and immutable presence is hiding. NIKOS KAZANTZAKIS

From soul to soul we send forth signals,
flashing our little suns,
waiting for answers that would join river to river
and all rivers to the sea. CATHERINE DE VINCK

Intellectual superiority brings men close to light. Holiness brings them close to Jesus Christ ERNEST HELLO

CHAPTER 7

THE MAN
OF DESIRE

THE SEARCH FOR GOD

BEFORE TRYING to reach a conclusion, let us summarize the situation of our present world in the light of what was said above. What is happening NOW is the passing from adolescent religiosity to an adult approach to the mystery of life. In earlier and more naive times, it was enough for the layman to memorize some simple dogmas and obey passively the commandments of God and his Church as expressed in manuals and explained by teachers and preachers. This led to a state of spiritual security compared to that of innocence before the fall : a good, smug, comfortable confidence in the absolute value of one's beliefs and practices, and distrust for anyone else's. When this was further enhanced by personal devotions, novenas, ways of the cross, venerations of relics and an accumulation of indulgences, one had the feeling of having done very well in terms of spiritual accounting. If the world was going to pots, it was none of our business. Comfort and assurance were carried over to Sunday Mass, where everyone was left to his own devices while the priest mumbled incomprehensible Latin to the wall.

But now, behold : people are getting involved in social and public issues, tenets are being reformulated, some saints turn out to have been imaginative frauds. Cherished practices from which merit had accrued suddenly drop out of sight. How can a Catholic be distinguished from a Protestant if both eat meat on Fridays? The Mass is no longer a free-for-all : people are expected to understand what is going on and to participate in it. The priest is no longer part of the church funishings, but has become a human being, one of the people, speaking to them face to face, offering their sacrifice together with them in a language all understand. Perhaps one day he will be allowed to marry : another earth-shaking scandal to the adolescent thinker. Perhaps also the Church will admit belatedly that its treatment of marriage and birth-control had been inconsiderate, unfounded and unreal—an apparent blow to infallibility.

Liberal Catholics are accused of throwing out the baby with the bathwater. In fact, some of them seem to be throwing out the sponge and the soap and the bathtub, and they are in imminent danger of throwing themselves out with all the rest. By contrast, the traditionalists refuse to throw out anything : they are carefully preserving the bathwater in sacred vessels. They want the status quo; they prefer the priest's back to the sight of his face, a dead language to a living one, the trivia and trimmings of a pagan renaissance court to an expression of simplicity and sincerity in the Liturgy, the pomp, pretense, hypocrisy an authoritarianism of ancient ways to any contemporary expression of our love for God.

The present crisis is not so much a crisis of faith as a crisis of honesty : authorities are faced with the obligation of admitting their own ignorance, while the faithful are faced with mystery which has uncomfortably replaced the passive security of earlier times. The credibility gap must be closed on both sides.

Things are not as dark as they may seem to be. We are living in the most exciting times of history, at the dawn of religious adulthood. We no longer accept being pushed around, forced by anyone to believe in verbal formulas. We no longer accept the principle that God can be analyzed and defined and contained in a book. We no longer submit to masters of the spiritual life : our spiritual life is our own. *With a newly awakened curiosity, with a healthy and intelligent skepticism that does not exclude the possibility of total faith, we forge ahead in our search for truth and love, leaving behind us a trail of ruined humbuggery.*

Many simple souls are upset by religious landslides and earthquakes the likes of which were never seen before. They are fully deserving of our sympathy and understanding, but our first duty is not to console the belated but to instruct them in the coming of what is good.

No, God is not dead : the God of Abraham, Isaac and Jacob is closer to us than he ever was. But God has ceased to be a glorified Monsignor. He is no longer Roman, nor Latin, nor Western; no longer a concept, but a reality of an entirely different order; he who Is, the mystery of mystery, and yet the Lover of Mankind closer to us than we are to ourselves.

The burden of mankind has been placed on a single pair of shoulders : those of the individual I. Day by day, or rather, instant by instant, I will achieve the salvation of the world and my own through a personal response to my personal challenge. All men have been entrusted to every one of us : none can be excluded from the compass of our love. We are bound in conscience to seek the welfare of all. Our prayers may extend to all, but our practical action is limited to those with whom we come into direct contact. Even they may be more numerous than appears at first sight : who can count the number of those affected by our writing, our speech or our example?

Communication, then, must be established with God and neighbor—with God through the neighbor, with God in the neighbor, for remember again, " the fat lady in Christ." The only thing we actually know of God is that which we see of him reflected in human love. Communication and commitment bring about communion, community, the social group, the gathering. This is the family, the *ecclesia*, that is called upon to express its common worship through a common Liturgy. It must be celebrated in such a way that it provides food for all. For the simple-minded, there must be clearly visible, material, obvious action : offering, incensing, singing. Then, there must be symbolical action, expressing worship, propitiation, thanksgiving. For worshipers concerned with anthropomorphism, there must be mythological action, attention being given to the saints and to personifications of virtues and divine attributes. For the metaphysically minded, there must be action expressing the one, the true and the good of the Trinity. For the mystics, there must be a reverent and faithful performance of the mystery of love. The Liturgy must be all things to all men, whatever the level of their mental or emotional development.

Do not be offended, then, if a church is full of statues, holy water fonts, stained glass windows and other paraphernalia. Perhaps you don't need them : others do. Perhaps you would prefer stark whitewashed walls and a slab of stone for an altar : others would see no religious spirit in such things. Perhaps you would prefer to attend Mass in the company of a chorus of impeccable angels instead of a mob of chattering and picturesquely garbed Arabs, moving in and out of the Church of St. Elias on Mount Carmel, sitting on the side-altar steps, noisily dragging chairs around, and rubbing silk kerchiefs with great devotion all over the statue of their beloved saint in the hope of receiving his protection—but this is true and living faith!

For *faith is fundamentally the act of man in his humanity and imperfection attempting to rise to the fullness of the promise.* Humanity is the keynote of every religious effort. It is also the door to our knowledge of God, for Jesus said, " He who sees me sees the Father. " Before the incarnation, believers had contact only with their prophets who in turn reached God only as a mysterious voice or symbolic manifestation. Since the birth of Christ in Bethlehem, man has received the incredible illumination of finding God within himself, by looking at the Prince of Peace in a stable, the Man of Sorrow dying on the cross, the Son of God rising on the third day and lifting all things up with him. We have not seen God in full, but we have seen in Christ how much of man is truly divine.

Christ came, not to destroy the law and the prophets, but to fulfill them. He came as a powerful and warm spring wind, scattering the dead leaves of a dead season : the ritualistic narrow-mindedness of the oppressing Scribes and Pharisees. And they—because they clung to their privileges and yielded not to the Spirit—were brushed away, ever to weep in their damaged pride over the ruins of the Holy City they themselves had destroyed. And the Spirit moved beyond them and settled on the humble of heart, Jews and Gentile; and it is of this Spirit that we breathe and live and have our being, and that the Church was born and stands forever, despite its enemies, despite what we ourselves so often do to cast it down.

Every time that—in the world and in religion—some practice takes precedence over charity, some man-made constitution stifles love, some scheme of perfection followed to the letter leaves the neighbor floundering, we are forgetting that the spring wind has come, that the letter is now dead while the Spirit lives. We are no better than the Scribes and the Pharisees, and with them we are again crucifying Christ.

The freedom of the children of God is this tremendous gift by which we live through love alone. " Love and do as you will ", said Augustine. You will then be doing the will of Love. *Obey God, but in the spirit of love, not as the punctilious slave of the word made master, but as the free and trusting child of the Word made flesh.* And this you should never forget : the Christ of Bethlehem and Nazareth, the Christ of the triumphal entry and of the agony in the garden the Christ of the crucifixion and the resurrection, is also the all-powerful Word and Son of God, the Alpha and Omega of creation, the First and Last in all things.

It is the same Christ, both man and God, who comes to us in a totally incomprehensible manner in the mystery of the Eucharist. This may well seem the most inacceptable, the most crude, the most revolting of all mysteries. Since the very beginning of Christianity, it has been a stumbling block for believers accused of eating their God. " Unless indeed you eat my body and drink my blood... " These are hard words : it takes a madman or God himself to utter them. How can a rational mind accept the plunge into such supra-rational folly? Is this not an abdication of its royal power? It would be, if there we no truth in Christ's teaching about himself. So this is the very point where every man and woman must decide. Every thinking man and woman at one time must become a convert. At this particular stage of thought, the offer is made to him either to trust Christ blindly, or refuse him.

THE ATHEIST

FOR THE MAN who refuses Christ, there may be nothing left but despair and meaninglessness. The world seems dominated by futility, leading to the belief that since nothing is worthwhile, anything goes : that there are no such things as moral law, civilization, love, decency, but only a desperate fight in which the leanest, the strongest and the least scrupulous win some few moments of pleasure or power.

The so-called emancipated end up in a form of slavery more strin-
gent and torturing than faith : for they become slaves to their own
folly and have no one to blame but themselves. The great prophets
of materialistic existentialism, acclaimed as leaders and liberators,
turn up at the end to be pitiful wrecks. In the latest volume of
the autobiography of Simone de Beauvoir, there is an expression
of whining and fretting surprise at the loss of her youth, a very
conventional and bourgeois concern over the decay of her image in
the mirror, and a frank avowal that she has been gypped : that the
values she had devoted her life to were false. Little more is left
of her than a lonely and confused old woman, she who had been the
shining example of liberated womanhood!

But what of the happy atheist? Of the man of honor who leads a
straight life by his own law, finding his reward in the rightness
of his will, proud of not having to depend upon the promise of some
vague future in order to live a life of dignity right now? Every
man is by nature religious : adoration of some absolute is part of
us. The materialistic existentialist worships his own freedom and
pleasure and reaps his own nothingness. The happy atheist also has
his God to whom he refuses to give a name. He may be more respectful of the absolute, more intellectually and morally honest than many
a pious soul whose total religion consists in the uncritical acceptance
of superstitious concepts. The professed atheist may be a man
who refuses to acknowledge a man-made and man-named God. But
even if he has no name for the reason of his life, he still is living
for the sake of some inner light, some idea of perfection he conceives
and obeys, otherwise he would jump into a river of oblivion, be
it water, alcohol, drugs, sex or some combination of them.

Whenever we see a happy atheist, a man of principles and deceny,
creative, warm, intelligent, alive, it would be dangerous to condemn
him to some theological hell. He may have found Christ without
daring to name him, accepting the law of love as his guide, while
seeing so little of this love in those who profess to live by it. Even if
he loudly rejects the notion of God, the divinity of Christ and every
other tenet of the Christian faith, perhaps his revolt is against
the formalization of such a faith, against its too human expression.

Bertrand Russell seems to have been such a man when he wrote
in his collection of essays " Why I Am Not a Christian " (1957) *

---

* Although Russell cannot be properly called an atheist.

We ought to make the best we can of the world, and if it is not so good as we wish, after all it will still be better than what these others have made of it in all these ages. A good world needs knowledge, kindliness and courage; it does not need a regretful hankering after the past or a fettering of the free intelligence by the words uttered long ago by ignorant men. It needs a fearless outlook and a free intelligence. It needs hope for the future, not looking back all the time toward a past that is dead, which we trust will be far surpassed by the future that our intelligence can create.

But there is, in the happy atheist, the very serious risk of the loner, the risk of pride and supercilious disregard for the faith of the hoi-polloi. In all matters, and particularly those of religion, humility in an essential virtue.

In the last paragraph of " The Idea of Christ in the Gospels, " George Santayana expresses beautifully the effect of the absence of Christ :

The idea of Christ crucified has had many worshipers, and has inspired many saints. But it has not converted the world or saved it. The world does not wish to be saved. If we say that the world thereby wills its own damnation, we are merely venting our private displeasure, without frightening the world. The flux of existence cannot be stopped by reflection. To stop may well seem to it a worse damnation than never to be able to stop. But in fact life is not condemned to either fate, because materially it always passes on, but in spirit it sometimes transcends into realisation of the eternal. There is aesthetic delight in this, as well as moral peace and intellectual clearness; but those who miss these things do not regret missing them. It would not be in the spirit of Christ to blame them for that privation : verily they have their reward. Yet, their reward, from the spiritual point of view, is itself their punishment, for it keeps them from ever understanding the power of their own minds or judging anything otherwise than by accidental passion.

Each one of us is a person, unique, valuable, irreplaceable in the universe. If we exist at all, it is because we are loved. Every man and woman is offered the opportunity to give and receive the bounty of love. The only condition is that they say YES.

Listening and seeking will consist essentially in a quest for God :
at first, a blind groping for the unknown, then the discovery of
the reasonably Absolute. Many rest there, but there is much beyond
this stage : the sudden pain of doubt, the absurdity of faith, the
total vacuum of absence which the mystics call the dark night
of the spirit. This may last for days or years—or even a lifetime.
Then, for the highly privileged, there are flashes of presence, the
discovery of the unnameable one, not as the other, but as that which
is deepest within them, the gratuitous and spontaneous, the fanciful
and beautiful, the gracious and surprising, the Living One.

That is truly what the man of desire is seeking. Call his search
faith or metaphysical hunger : no *thing* is good enough to satisfy so
deep a craving, except all that is. Is such hunger a curse or a gift?
It deprives the subject of contentment but not of peace, of satisfaction but not of pleasure. It keeps him ever-alert, ready for the next
step forward, the next crossing of a spiritual river, the next climbing
of a mystical hill. For him, the river and the hill are not mere stages
of a self-sufficient reality, but the signs and conditions of what
is to follow. For the man of desire, pain becomes merit, and pleasure
is an imperfect symbol of what he seeks. Nothing is too hard and
nothing good enough. He stands above anything that may happen
to him, towering over his fate, over the pattern of his everyday life.
To him, all this is not an end, but a beginning : one more
step forward in the search for all.

God is not only our final state, but also, and permanently, our deepest nature, absent from us only insofar as we absent ourselves from him and linger in the superficial regions of our soul. SUZANNE LILAR

EPILOGUE

ALONG THE MOVING PATHS of every sea, in raging storm or windless calm, in the blazing sun or under distant stars, the ancient mariners followed the song of the sirens... and they drowned. We, too, have such dreams of sweet and silent paradise, of a green depth of delight, and we set sail for distant isles, and with pounding hearts and wide amazed eyes, we drown like the mariners of old without having been told the name of our desire.

We often believe that happiness and peace are just beyond the bluest range of mountains; and because our heart is a wanderer and our spirit a spirit of unrest, we leave the safe refuge of even days and stretch out our wings to follow the wild goose over the hills and far away. Alas, beyond the hills are other hills and seas uncounted. After many labors and after many days, we find ourselves returned to our familiar void, and still we do not know the name of our desire.

So off we go to plumb the depths of life, seeking some food for what we cannot kill, seeking throughout the cities of the world that ecstasy that would be all in all. Down into the folds of our instinctive bodies we delve and dive and drown and drown again until we sink into the darkness of despair.

" O life, where is thy beauty? What of thy words and promises so fair? Where is the all-enfolding passion that quenches thirst and stills immortal hunger?" Alas, we do not even know the name of our desire.

And all the while, along the sun's bright glory, along the silent wonders of the moon, there breathes one whose name is love, the long-forgotten name of our desire.

" O Lord of seas and mountains, O Lord of love, have mercy on us who cry out to thee. Perhaps the ways of our search were strange and tortured : often and most unwisely did we sin. But even though we did believe in other loves than thine, what is love outside of thee? Beyond the seas, over the mountains, more than power or wealth, more than the humble warmth of human flesh, was it not thee, O Lord, that we were seeking? Didst thou not hide among our earthly splendors, and did we not in our blind and clumsy way give our hearts to thee?

" But now, O Lord, that thou hast spoken, now that we know the name of our desire, inflame our fragile love, clutch it between thy golden claws and lift us trembling to the splendor of thy sun. "

APPENDIX

The Mystery of God according to St. Bonaventure of Bagnorea

" Good is said to be self-diffusive; therefore the highest good is that which diffuses itself the most. Now, diffusion cannot stand as the highest unless it is intrinsic yet actual, substantial yet personal, essential yet voluntary, neccessary yet free, perfect yet incessant. Thus, in the supreme good there must be from all eternity an actual and consubstantial producing, the producing of a hypostasis as noble as the One who produces by way of both generation and spiration. * So there is produced an Eternal Principle, who is an eternal Co-producer. And thus, there is the producing of one Beloved and one Co-beloved, of one begotten and one spirated. So in all there are the Father, the Son and the Holy Spirit. Otherwise, this good could not be supreme, since it would not be supremely self-diffusive. For truly, compared to the immensity of eternal goodness, diffusion in time as manifested in creation is nothing but a point without dimensions. Hence, it is possible to think of a greater diffusion, to wit, one through which the diffusing subject communicates to the object the totality of its substance and nature. Therefore, good would not be supreme if either in the order of reality or in the order of reason it lacked this perfect diffusion.

" If, therefore, you are able to behold with your mental vision this pure goodness which is the pure act of a Principle who loves with the love of charity, such love being both gratuitous and due, and a combination of both, such pure goodness is an absolute diffusion in both essence and will. It is a diffusion by way of the Word in whom all things are expressed, and by way of the Gift by whom all other gifts are given. Should you, then, be able to see with the eyes of your mind this pure goodness, you can also see that its

---

* Generation is the method through which the Son is begotten by the Father; spiration, that through which the Holy Spirit is breathed by the Father and the Son.

supreme communicability necessarily postulates the trinity of Father, Son and Holy Spirit. Since goodness is supreme in them, so must communicability be; since communicability is supreme, so must consubstantiality be; since consubstantiality is supreme, so must alikeness be, which necessitates supreme coequality, and this, in turn, supreme coeternity; while all the attributes together necessitate supreme mutual indwelling, each Person existing necessarily in the others by supreme circumincession, and each acting with the others in utter indivision of substance, power and operation in this most blessed Trinity.

" But while studying these matters, beware of thinking that you comprehend the incomprehensible : for, concerning these six attributes, there are other things to consider that will lead our mental vision to the height of rapt admiration. Here, indeed, is supreme communicability together with individuality of Persons; supreme consubstantility with hypostatic plurality; supreme alikeness with distinct personality; supreme coequality with successively ordered origin; supreme coeternity with emanation; supreme indwelling with emission. Who would not be lifted up in wonder at the sight of such marvels? Yet, if we raise our eyes to the supremely excellent goodness we can understand with complete certainty that all this is found in the most blessed Trinity. If, indeed, there is present here supreme communication together with true diffusion, there is also true origination and true distinction; and since the whole is communicated, and not only a part, the very same is given that is possessed, and that, in its entirety. Therefore, the One emanating and the One producing are both distinguished by their properties and in essence one. Because distinguished by their properties, they have personal properties, a plurality of hypostases, emanation as a manner of origination, sequence, not of one after the other but of one from the other, and emission, * not in terms of physical displacement, but through free spiration based on the producer's authority : the authority which the sender has over the one who is sent. But because they are truly one in substance, they must be one in essence, form, dignity, eternity, existence, and unlimitedness.

" If you consider these things one by one, in themselves, they

* Not all that is said here applies to all three Persons. Emanation is proper to the Son and to the Holy Spirit, and emission, to the Father in relation to the Son, while spiration is proper to the Father in relation to the Holy Spirit.

are enough to give you a vision of the truth. If you consider them in relation to one another, they are enough to suspend you in the deepest wonder. Therefore, if you wish to rise mentally through wonder to wondering contemplation, you should consider them together." *

*" The Works of Bonaventure," translated from the Latin by José de Vinck, vol. I, " Mystical Opuscula," pp. 49-52 (The Journey of the Mind to God) St. Anthony Guild Press, Paterson, N.J. 1960.

INDEX

19 74

Printed by GEDIT S.A.

Tournai, Belgium

Set in Times Roman

SECOND PRINTING

Designed and Decorated
by the Author